YES WE HAVE NO BANANAS

Outdoor Relief in Belfast
1920–39

D1357708

YES WE HAVE NO BANANAS

Outdoor Relief in Belfast
1920–39

Paddy Devlin

Blackstaff Press

British Library Cataloguing in Publication Data

Devlin, Paddy
  Yes, we have no bananas: Outdoor Relief in
  Belfast 1920–1939.
  1. Public Welfare – Northern Ireland – Belfast
  2. Belfast – Poor
  362.5'8'094167   HV250.B/

  ISBN 0–85640–246–X

Printed in Northern Ireland by W & G Baird Limited

Contents

Preface

Paul Bew

This is a book about a wretchedly inhuman system – the administration of Outdoor Relief in Belfast from 1920 to 1939. It opens a window on the harshness of the Depression of the Thirties in the city. It is perhaps especially appropriate that it should be published in 1981, when Belfast is again facing unemployment levels which remind us of those dark days.

Yes We Have No Bananas may seem to be a strange title for a history book. Yet it is, in fact, a suitable and revealing one. It points us to that dramatic moment in Belfast's history when in October 1932 the city resounded not to the sound of sectarian or party tunes but to a simple refrain which yet had an enormous potential political significance. Is the unity of the Belfast working class, historically divided by bitter religious antagonisms, ever possible? The Outdoor Relief crisis of 1932 – provoked by the harshness of the Outdoor Relief system – tells us unambiguously that it is. As Paddy Devlin demonstrates here, Catholic and Protestant workers did come together in a successful struggle to raise relief rates. Yet, as he also points out, the musical heritage on both sides reflected the traditional Orange and Green divisions. And so it was that 'Yes We Have No Bananas' – the only neutral tune available – became Belfast's anthem of progress.

The working-class unity of 1932 did not last long. We still need to know a great deal more about these problems in the history of our labour movement. The author here contributes his own interpretation of the rise in sectarian feeling which culminated in the riots of 1935. This will provoke much debate among those interested in such matters.

This is Paddy Devlin's first book since his account of the fall of the power-sharing Executive in Northern Ireland in 1974. (He was of course, a prominent Minister in that Executive.) Since his resignation from the SDLP, Mr Devlin has in recent years been concerned with the construction of non-sectarian Socialist politics in Belfast. Along the way he has had to deal with some pretty tough problems. Nevertheless, he has been able to play a role, along with other brave and generous forces, in bringing about some broad-based alliances in the city council on economic and social matters.

This is a polemical and passionate work by a man who is an active Socialist and full-time trade union organiser. The truth is that until very recently ignorance of the history of the Northern Ireland state was almost frightening. Our knowledge of working-class Belfast in the inter-war period is still slight. Through his involvement in the Northern Ireland Labour Party Paddy Devlin has had a unique access to the recollections of the labour movement activists, both Protestant and Catholic. This has enabled him to produce an inimitable and fascinating account of the fortunes of labour between the wars. The book is based on much extensive research. The author has worked his way through many of the Parliamentary Debates, Cabinet files and newspapers of the period. He has a strong feel for the wider currents of Irish history. He has read the products of the most recent academic scholarship – though he does not always agree with the views he has found there. He has presented all this in a lively and attractive manner. While much work remains to be done on the history of Belfast, Mr Devlin has placed us in his debt.

List of Abbreviations

ITGWU	Irish Transport and General Workers' Union
NAUL	National Amalgamated Union of Labour
NILP	Northern Ireland Labour Party
NUDL	National Union of Dock Labourers
NUWM	National Unemployed Workers' Movement
PR	Proportional Representation
RIC	Royal Irish Constabulary
TUC	Trades Union Conference
UPL	Ulster Protestant League
UULA	Ulster Unionist Labour Association
UWM	Unemployed Workers' Movement

Introduction

This is the story of the Outdoor Relief system as administered in Belfast from 1920, when the Northern Ireland Government was established, until the abolition of that system in 1939. Unlike its existence and development in Britain, where changes were effected by public pressure to achieve justice for millions who were suffering intense poverty, hunger and destitution, different motives wrought different changes throughout its life in Ireland.

Four themes run through the story: (1) the attempts made by the Belfast bourgeoisie to contain the growth of Catholics and labour supporters in the latter part of the nineteenth century and more particularly from 1920 onwards; (2) the separation of workers on a sectarian basis; (3) the abortion of class politics and the consequent success of Unionism; (4) the alienation of both sections of the working class by the Poor Law Guardians whose zeal in carrying out their duties led to extensive rioting in 1932 and ultimately to their replacement for corruption in 1939.

Unionists always worked to a loose strategy which was built into the new institutions when they took over the reins of government. From 1921, the strategy became firm and was applied comprehensively. It was extended into job and relief-deprivation as well as into the sphere of electoral equality. It was to be the key to their maintaining political control henceforth in Northern Ireland.

The social policy of the Northern Ireland Government at the outset was directed towards forcing Catholics and labour supporters to emigrate or reduce the size of their families by economic deprivation. This policy was maintained for the first twenty years of the Government's life even though the Poor Law was abolished in England in 1928 and in the Free State in 1924.

From 1931 onwards, all social security legislation introduced in Northern Ireland was amended to retain the principle of discretion in

1

the administration of relief to the needy. It was agreed between the Government of England and of Northern Ireland in 1925 that this legislation would be on a parity basis. In England it operated on the basis that the able-bodied unemployed had an entitlement to cash benefit. This was not the case in Northern Ireland. Administrators of social services, including the Poor Law Guardians, interpreted the Acts in a way that gave political preference to Government supporters.

This story tells how Outdoor Relief was applied by the Belfast Poor Law Guardians to the needy; how, at first, they followed faithfully the direction set out for them by the Unionist Party leadership only to allow themselves to be diverted from that strategy afterwards by their own instinctive and petty hatred of the poor.

The story is based on a thesis which has been submitted for academic distinction. The material contained in it has been written up after a detailed examination of Reports of Parliamentary Debates, Cabinet Minutes, Poor Law Guardians' Records and Minutes, newspaper reports and interviews with public representatives and others who, like myself, lived through the period. One prominent Government official to whom I spoke on the subject requested that his name be withheld.

Names, terms and descriptions vary constantly throughout the text because of the time-span covered and the changing patterns of related events. Catholic and Protestant are the basic terms. In some contexts, Catholics become the Minority, the Nationalists or, indeed, Sinn Feiners, while Protestants are described as Orangemen, the Majority, or the Unionists. At times these descriptions have been stretched to cover Protestants as skilled craft union members or the 'aristocracy of labour' and Catholics as unskilled, able-bodied unemployed or members of the general labouring unions. The term 'across the water', which is used throughout the book, is a basic Unionist euphemism, meaning to convey the impression that Unionists live on the same land mass but separated by an inconvenient pool of water. I have kept to this term, however inaccurate, to avoid confusion.

Part I

1
Unionist Strategy and Structures

The Unionist strategy for controlling the wealth and resources, as well as the political institutions of Northern Ireland, took two forms: in the pre-partition period it was based on a crude expression of Orange power, and in the post-partition period it was replaced by a more subtle management of state agencies and institutions. This study is about how the bourgeoisie merged these two forms into a single strategy to take control and maintain their political hegemony of Belfast in particular and of the North in general.

During the nineteenth century the bourgeoisie of Belfast gradually organised themselves, the Orange Order, the Protestant churches, local government representatives and their election machine, into a tight Unionist coalition that maintained its ascendancy through discrimination, patronage and fear of real or imagined bogymen such as the spectre of Home Rule, Popery or a high Catholic birthrate.[1]

This coalition, which formalised itself into the Unionist Party after the turn of the century, clearly devised a pattern of discrimination against Catholics which, in the face of frequent rioting, forced them to retreat into ghettoes where their voting strength at the ballot box would be impotent. Moreover, by keeping Catholics within the confines of their ghettoes it was comparatively easy to deprive them of jobs and to restrict the number of houses available for them to live in. However, a more subtle but effective weapon in the Unionist arsenal was applied when the Catholic families sought relief from hunger. The Poor Law Guardians, having the power to exercise discretion as to who should be relieved, refused to assist those they believed to be intruders on the natives of Belfast. To achieve this objective the capacity to relieve distress in Belfast was severely limited compared to other cities of similar size and character elsewhere in Britain.

Some sections of the Unionist coalition felt more hostility towards Catholics than others: sometimes the feeling against them was more bitter than at other times. These were occasions when the Home Rule Bills were under debate at Westminster: usually rioting of a protracted nature ensued, resulting in the loss of Catholic lives. Generally, skilled workers in membership of the Orange Order fiercely resented the presence outside the factory gates of unemployed navvies from the south or west of Ireland who had come there seeking work. Employers, of course, were not slow to exploit their presence to keep wages down and to remind Orangemen at election time of their duty to keep the rural invaders at bay.

In 1921, after the Unionists were established in office, the pattern of discrimination and deprivation was cemented into the affairs of the new institutions of government. With this new power, discrimination was intensified by the Unionists and became even more effective.

Whereas before 1921 discrimination in employment was applied to Catholics only, it was now applied to those Protestants who supported the cause of labour. The key to how it was done lay entirely in the hands of the Government's administrators. The unemployed worker needed unemployment insurance payments or Outdoor Relief to keep him and his family alive. To be entitled to the former, constant short-term employment was needed; to receive the latter, relieving officers had to recommend to the Poor Law Guardians that the person concerned was worthy of it. Either way the Unionists determined whether or not a term of employment was arranged or Outdoor Relief granted. The 'crunch' was usually reached when both were refused, as usually happened to Catholics and labour supporters. They were then faced with the choice of limiting their families and living in circumstances of extreme humiliation and starvation, or emigrating to wherever the relieving officer would pay the fare. This was the essence of Unionist strategy – to make the conditions so hard for their opponents that they had no alternative but to leave the country, and to make it sufficiently comfortable for their supporters that they would stay.

The end of the First World War brought a complication that had the potential to wreck the Unionist strategy. It took the form of a growing Labour Party that threatened to create new political alignments as well as social and economic issues of a more radical character than Unionists had had to contend with to date – an economic depression, getting deeper every year, made that party alarmingly relevant.

Catholic politics the Unionists could handle but labour politics, inspired mainly by Protestant workers, they regarded as the 'kiss of death'. From then onwards the Labour Party, as well as the Catholics, were regarded as enemies within the gates and were treated as such by the state's representatives.

So it came to pass; Labour candidates and their agents as well as the traditional enemies were beaten up at each election. Proportional representation, written into the Government of Ireland Act 1920, was abolished for local government and Northern Ireland elections – to keep elections on a purely Catholic and Protestant basis. The reason behind the abolition of PR was to keep the Labour Party from getting advantages from a second preference vote that would 'blur the issues and confuse the electorate'.

Discrimination, and the deprivation of jobs, houses and social benefits, now official Government policy, were underpinned by the existence of a Special Powers Act and special auxiliary policemen – in Belfast mainly comprised of Orange shipyard workers. The Act, which was aimed at the survival of the Unionist state, was used freely against Catholics and occasionally against labour supporters.

There was no ambiguity about the Unionist Government's position on class issues. They unequivocally represented the interest of big business and the landowning gentry to the total exclusion of all other matters. Many of them were elected because of their feudal-baron status by rural workers who accepted an existence that was the equal of medieval serfs. The big landowners and manufacturers owned their workers, lock, stock and barrel, and ran, without demur, as unopposed candidates in each election. They had neither cause with, nor care for, the local people they purported to represent. Dissent from their political policies brought the stigma of 'Rotten Prod' or of 'disloyalty to the Crown' on the head of those who did not vote for them, in addition to the loss of a job and a home. For example, of the seven Ministers in the first Unionist Cabinet of 1921, three were former presidents of the Chamber of Commerce, one was a senior partner in the leading firm of company solicitors; of the other three, one was an industrialist, one a director of a number of companies, and one a titled owner of one of the largest estates in Northern Ireland.[2] The class composition of the 1932 Cabinet was equally class biassed.

The Unionist Government, like the Party itself, represented the interests of big business. While the explicit objective of the Party was the maintenance of the Union between Northern Ireland and Britain, the affairs of government showed an increasing engagement with controlling the Opposition because it was feared that the Socialists,

Table 1

Members of Northern Ireland Government, October 1932[3]

Prime Minister	Lord Craigavon	Whiskey Distiller
Minister of Finance	Hugh Pollock	Company Director
Minister of Commerce	John Milne Barbour	Linen Manufacturer
Chief Whip	Captain Herbert Dixon	Importer & Landowner
Minister of Home Affairs	Sir R. Dawson Bates	Company Director & Lawyer
Minister of Labour	John Andrews	Linen Manufacturer
Minister of Education	Viscount Charlemont	Landowner & Company Director
Minister of Agriculture	Sir Edward Archdale	Extensive Landowner
Attorney General	A. Babington	King's Counsel
Speaker	Henry Mulholland	Linen Manufacturer & Company Director

given the chance, would expropriate their factories and their wealth.

Certainly, the Government Ministers were strong supporters of the private enterprise system and believed completely in freedom of market-place forces to set profits and prices for Northern Ireland's regional economy. The Ministers saw it as perfectly normal to extend their private interests into control over government institutions. After all, who else could be trusted to do it? Had the Ministers not more knowledge and experience in the affairs of big business than anyone else? Was not government of a country the same as government of a business concern on a larger and more diffuse scale?

In reality, the Government Ministers were small-minded, myopic men whose claims to office were based more on their abilities as sectarian warriors than on their distinguished business acumen. Indeed, Lord Londonderry remarked in 1922 of a Cabinet colleague, Sir Dawson Bates, that his previous work was no training for his duties as Home Secretary and his standing in the country was not high enough to run successfully a government office. Lord Londonderry was probably right about Bates. Bates was reported in 1927 to have refused to suspend the Belfast Corporation when corruption in housing contracts was discovered. He said to a disbelieving audience, 'The subsequent unpopularity may have led to the spread of Socialism.' Lord Londonderry left in disgust in 1925 after condemning the Government's pre-occupation with one thought – that of maintaining the Union with Britain.[4] An overall view of Cabinet records for the period tends to support Lord Londonderry's view of his erstwhile colleagues. They did seem to be incapable of absorbing enough of the simple facts of business life to enable them to plan for Northern Ireland's future. They concentrated almost entirely on creating tension and sectarian dissension within the community at the cost of driving away outside investment and causing the young, able and educated, around whom Northern Ireland's industrial regeneration should have been built, to flee the country in shame.

It would be wrong to state that the Unionist Government had no political cunning or guile. There is evidence that they had an abundance of both when they succeeded in removing Westminster restraint from their political affairs.

James Craig, the Prime Minister, introduced a Local Government Bill to abolish Proportional Representation in local elections. It was unopposed in Parliament, the Irish Nationalist MPs abstaining at the time, and passed all stages of the procedure by 5 July 1922. The Bill was aimed at depriving Catholic representatives of their fair share of local administration. It cut across the provisions of the Government of Ireland Act 1920 and was considered by the British Government to be *ultra vires* the Act. Royal Assent was consequently delayed.

Craig and his Cabinet met on 27 July and decided to resign as a body unless the Bill received the Royal Assent immediately. Their resignation statement contained the following sentence: 'To allow this precedent to be created would warrant the interference by the Imperial Government in almost every Act introduced in Northern Ireland.'

It was a fundamental crisis that could have ended Westminster's hopes of a settlement in the rest of Ireland as well as in the North. The British Government backed down and Royal Assent was given on 11 September. On several occasions afterwards, when issues of a similar nature arose and were deemed to be in breach of the Government of Ireland Act 1920, such as the Education Acts of 1925 and 1930, the Home Office in London made only token efforts to amend them. It was a clear-cut victory for the Unionists and it ensured that they could run the affairs of Northern Ireland according to their own lights.

The victory enabled the Unionists, once they had a ballot-box majority, to impose their will on the minority without regard to the essentials of democracy or the necessity for a pendulum effect in the political control of the administration.

9

Meanwhile, relationships within the Cabinet were far from perfect. Two minor ideologies had developed within the Northern Ireland Government which are usefully defined by other historians as populism and anti-populism.

The populists were led by the Prime Minister, James Craig, and supported by the Minister of Home Affairs, R. Dawson Bates; the Minister of Labour, J.M. Andrews; and the Chief Whip, Herbert Dixon. The anti-populists were led by Hugh Pollock who was Minister of Finance and Deputy Prime Minister; the Minister of Commerce, John Milne Barbour; and Sir Wilfrid Spender, Permanent Secretary of the Ministry of Finance, promoted in 1925 to head of the Civil Service.[5]

The populists sought to keep support intact for the Unionist Party by providing, from the public purse, a generous flow of patronage and 'perks' to selected groups. Anti-populists, for equally unworthy motives, sought to oppose this policy. The collision of policy is neatly summarised by Spender in a note which he made in his diary in 1931. He recorded that the Prime Minister had told him that whatever happened he expected the Ministry of Finance to provide a surplus which would be available for special local purposes; that he believed in the policy of 'distributing bones' and thought that they ought to be able to arrange with the British Government that funds were available for this purpose.[6]

The Government was tied by Cabinet resolution to a policy of parity with Westminster on matters of unemployment insurance and social services. Craig, speaking in Parliament as early as 14 March 1922, gave an unassailable commitment to MPs: 'It will never be said that workers in our midst worked under conditions worse than those across the water... where employment and benefits are concerned; it will be the Minister of Labour's duty to see that a man is treated as well on this side of the water.'[7] Andrews in the same debate hardened the commitment when he said that they would not carry on in government unless the workers enjoyed the same standards as across the water. They were both afraid that failure to maintain equal standards in social services would cause the workers to turn against them.[8]

The interesting point about these speeches was the constant references made in them to the workers. Unionist mythology had it that only their supporters ever wanted to work: opposition, both Catholic and labour, was made up of malingerers who had no jobs and did not want to work. They were not workers within the Unionist definition, therefore they were not qualified to receive the social service benefits. It was this specific theory that was the basis for their attempts to curtail entitlement to benefits to certain sections of workers while forcing the rest of the unemployed to seek help from the Poor Law Guardians, who applied politically-inspired discretion to the relief given.

Craig's fears of what effect inequality in social services between Northern Ireland and Britain would have on Unionist supporters was probably right. He returned to the theme after the general election in 1925 when Labour had won three seats in Belfast. He told Lord Londonderry that the failure of his government to follow West-minster's lead in not abolishing the Thrift Disqualification clause of the Old Age Pension Act was to blame for the loss of three seats to Labour. This clause had been amended in 1924 at Westminster to enable old age pensioners to save up to £39 per single person and £78 per married couple without loss of benefit. Pollock had prevailed on the Cabinet not to amend the Act. 'The effect of this action', said Craig, 'would really be infinitesimal compared with what would follow our getting out of step in regard to unemployment insurance.'[9]

He was still on the same theme the following month when he told his brother, in the face of an anti-populist move to stop the introduction of contributory pensions for the aged that

> the screw would be put on if we refuse to give the same benefits to people living in our own area... and that as we had adopted that attitude there was no necessity for our financial affairs to be so adjusted that we could live *pari passu* with the English and Scotch in other directions.[10]

The anti-populists, if less vocal, were more effective in keeping social expenditure down. They never accepted that parity on these matters was an article of faith. Even after the Colwyn Committee recommendation that there should be parity in social service spending had been accepted in Parliament in 1925, this group successfully resisted its implementation.

It was clear that Pollock and his Ministry officials accepted the view that too much money was being spent on social services and that the revenue collected from the employers as taxes was crippling, but his objection to spending money on social services was more broadly based than that. He was opposed ideologically to state intervention in social and economic affairs and believed that because earnings in Northern Ireland were lower than in Britain the level of social service

11

expenditure in Northern Ireland should correspond to the lower earnings.

This policy of the Ministry of Finance was set out with sobering clarity by Spender in a letter which he wrote to the Cabinet Secretary on 23 January 1931 on the issue of government help to relieve the critical unemployment situation. He stated that the workers were better off than in 1913 when there was no talk of acute distress. 'No wonder', he argued, 'that United Kingdom industries are finding it difficult to compete in world markets against those countries where taxation is so much less than with us and where wages have been dramatically reduced. The only remedy is to return to the days of lower taxation, lower wages and less state responsibility.'[11]

The result of this approach – which was not a subject of Cabinet conflict – was that every social benefit, including unemployment, fell behind those that were paid in Britain.

Dissatisfaction with this performance by the Government grew within the Unionist Party, particularly from the Ulster Unionist Labour Association. This dissatisfaction was best demonstrated by the increased number of divisions called in Parliament against the Government on social service legislation. In the first four years of Parliament's existence there was no MP on the Opposition benches. The number of divisions at this time rose from 20 per year in 1921 to 497 by 1925. William Grant, a fanatical Protestant MP who worked as a tradesman in the Belfast shipyard, was forced to vote against his own Government on social welfare issues on twenty-nine occasions.[12]

It was no surprise that the workers, skilled and unskilled, reacted at times to the Ministry of Finance's failure to provide step-by-step unemployment insurance benefits for them.

The unemployment insurance chart set out on p.13 describes how in a period of ten years the insured population of Great Britain increased by 5 per cent while that of Northern Ireland rose only marginally. But payments from the Exchequer to the general and insured population of Northern Ireland and Great Britain over the same period rose by 50 per cent for Northern Ireland compared with 1000 per cent for Great Britain. Yet a parity arrangement which was initiated on a recommendation of the Colwyn Committee the year before was totally ignored. Cash payments to the unemployed, which should have been paid on a pound-for-pound basis, were reduced to a shilling in the pound for Northern Ireland's unemployed.

Table 2
Unemployment Insurance 1926–1935[13]

Year ending 31 March		General population 1000s	Insured population 1000s	Insured population as % of general population	Exchequer payments to unemployment funds & transitional payments £	Exchequer Payments per head of general population £ s. d.	per head of insured population £ s. d.
1926:	GB	43,783	11,500	26.26	6,822,027	3. 1.	11. 10.
	NI	1,257	266	21.16	1,164,599	18. 6.	4 7. 7.
1927:	GB	43,964	11,630	26.50	10,837,821	4. 11.	18. 7.
	NI	1,254	263	20.97	1,515,371	7 4. 2.	5 15. 3.
1932:	GB	44,831	12,370	27.57	49,612,532	1 2. 2.	4 0. 3.
	NI	1,251	270	21.58	1,611,167	1 5. 9.	5 19. 4.
1933:	GB	45,084	12,400	27.50	79,331,282	15. 2.	6 7. 11.
	NI	1,262	265	21.00	1,901,903	1 10. 2.	7 3. 6.
1934:	GB	45,262	12,473	27.55	71,931,770	1 11. 9.	5 15. 4.
	NI	1,271	263	20.69	1,879,336	1 9. 7.	7 2. 11.
1935:	GB	45,446	12,540	27.59	66,850,000	1 9. 5.	5 6. 7.
	NI	1,280	268	20.94	1,864,000	1 9. 2.	6 19. 1.

That extraordinary differential over the stated period of ten years was no clerical error. Instead it was a deliberately calculated and comprehensive policy by the Department of Finance not to apply parity on insurance payments to Northern Ireland's unemployed. They had two reasons for departing from parity: it helped employers to trade competitively in the British markets by fixing wage levels to correspond with lower unemployment insurance benefits; and it allowed the Government and the Poor Law Guardians to use discretion in their selection of those entitled to relief. Apart from securing these two short-term objectives the Government had secured a first-rate mechanism to implement their overall strategy.

Why and how did it work? It worked because Pollock and the anti-populists were diametrically opposed to social services and refused to keep in step with British legislation in any case. The populists acquiesced because they were concerned only with skilled workers and those other unskilled workers who supported the Unionist Government. Unionist supporters, when unemployed, were all assisted within the framework of the Northern Ireland social service legislation. British legislation, which was part of the parity arrangement, was specifically amended in Northern Ireland to help them achieve that purpose.

Those Government supporters who failed to receive social service benefits and fell through the legislation cracks received help when they were caught in the Outdoor Relief net. The anti-Unionists, on the other hand, who were denied social service benefit due to long-term unemployment and forced to apply for Outdoor Relief, were subject to the discretion, rarely exercised in their favour, of the Poor Law Guardians. This study shows in the later chapters how the Poor Law Guardians applied their 'discretion' to anti-Unionists, and the consequences of this application.

2
Earlier Struggles of Catholics in Belfast

This study relates to the administration of Outdoor Relief and the way in which the Belfast Poor Law Guardians applied it to destitute Catholics and, to a much lesser extent, to destitute Protestants who refused to support Unionist rule. As Catholics are the focal point of the study it is necessary to paint a background of their origins in Belfast as well as describing the tensions, the strains and the persecution to which they were subject up to 1920.

In the early eighteenth century the native Irish, who were Catholic, were forced to live outside the city walls of Belfast by the Anglo-Scottish settlers who had been brought into Ulster in the wake of the Elizabethan wars. The Catholic families had concentrated on the west flank of the Lagan valley but later that century moved to the north and west corners of Belfast.

There seems little evidence of tension between the town inhabitants and the Catholics who were still subject to the rigours of Cromwell's Penal Code. Indeed the evidence that does exist points to the contrary. Sources in the Public Record Office indicate that the town's Presbyterians, the dominant religion, were mainly responsible for the building of the first Catholic chapel in Belfast. The town Volunteers, exclusively Presbyterian, formed a guard of honour at the opening and were to the forefront of popular agitation for the repeal of the Penal Laws.

During the previous two centuries Belfast had developed differently from the rest of Ireland. It was industrialised where the rest of Ireland was not. It was attracted to the economy of mainland Britain where the rest of Ireland was less so. Its population was different in culture and religious beliefs to the rest of Ireland. Its relations with the rest of Ireland were governed mainly by suspicion and at times a feeling of superior detachment. The relationship of Belfast's Catholics to the rest of its citizens was essentially different from those in any other Irish city. Around the earlier part of the nineteenth century Belfast expanded its industries in line with British growth, looking towards Scotland in particular for its coal and iron, its skilled and other key workers; and to Scottish financial institutions for capital and credit.

The first official head count of the population is given in the report of the Royal Commission of Public Institutions in 1834. The total population was reported as 60,813, of which 19,712 were Catholics. An earlier report in 1808 put the number of Catholics at 4,000 which represented 16 per cent of the population. There was a steady growth in the Catholic portion of the population until it reached 34 per cent around the 1850s.

Population figures for Belfast from 1861 until 1926 show a clear percentage decrease of Catholics from 34 to 23 per cent. The percentage remained static until the beginning of the Second World War when it began quite perceptibly to rise again. This rise was due to the availability of work, and increased with a more generous flow of relief and cash benefits after 1945 which resulted in a reduced number of emigrants, and the disappearance of sectarian rioting from Belfast. These figures tell the story of Unionist successes throughout the years 1920–39 in keeping the Catholic population from increasing. It was only the wartime economy, full employment and entitlement to the generous welfare benefits of the post-war Labour Government that caused the Catholic population figures to increase. Thus the strategy fashioned by the Unionist Government worked effectively in keeping down the Catholic population of Belfast prior to the 1940s.

As Belfast began to expand rapidly from the 1830s onwards, industries needed labour which was not readily available from the immediate areas. Catholics from the south and west of Ireland were attracted to fill the jobs created by the growing linen trade which lay mainly to the west and north of the city. It was to exploit the cheap labour available in that area that in 1838 Belfast entrepreneurs built the first railway link with Sligo in the west of Ireland.

Within a few years thousands of raw, uneducated Catholic labourers had poured into the city, increasing dramatically their numbers in proportion to the rest of the population. The industrial growth of Belfast coincided with rural depopulation which in the nineteenth century was highest between the famine years of the late Forties to the early Sixties. The immigrants were not townsfolk and knew little of townsfolk's habits – and they came from areas which were predominantly Catholic.[1]

16

Table 3
Roman Catholics in Belfast Population, 1808–1957
(Census of Ireland and Census of Northern Ireland figures)

Date	Number of Roman Catholics	Catholic % of total population
1808	4,000	16.0
1834	19,712	32.0
1861	41,406	33.9
1871	55,575	31.9
1881	59,975	28.8
1891	67,378	26.3
1901	84,994	24.3
1911	93,243	24.1
1926	95,682	23.0
1937	104,372	23.8
1957	115,029	25.9

These figures were extracted from sources in the Public Record Office of Northern Ireland.

Belfast city-dwellers were Protestant by religion and Scottish in character. Over the years they had acquired artisan skills. Their religion, speech and industrial habits were the direct opposite to those of the uncouth intruders whom they regarded as competitors for their jobs and homes. They had developed their own brand of puritan ethic in education, literature, morality and living standards.[2] The belief that worldly riches were a positive sign of God's approbation dominated their working lives,[3] and this belief was reinforced by the strict teachings of their church leaders.

The bourgeoisie were not slow to promote this ideology amongst their employees in the factories and in domestic and public affairs. Theories of religious, social and cultural inferiorities were grist to their mill and they applied them to all relationships. Those who did not support these virtues were treated as social lepers. It did not seem to matter that, materially, the immigrants were in no position to practise these virtues when they were entirely preoccupied with keeping themselves alive after fleeing from the ravages of rural famine.

A decisive link in the chain between the bourgeoisie and their workers was the Orange Order. Practically all were members or supporters. The Orange Order's objectives, aggressively anti-Catholic and strongly loyal to the Established Church and to the Crown, transcended everything.

This alliance has been referred to as a 'Corporatist ideology' and the following lines from an Orange song offered as evidence:

> Against the altar and the throne
> the democrat may prate,
> But while I am an Orangeman,
> I'll stand for Church and State.
>
> Let not the poor man hate the rich,
> nor rich on poor look down
> But each join each true Protestant
> for God and for the Crown.[4]

This religious ideology pursued by the bourgeoisie and supported by the Orange Order on the factory floor separated the Belfast labour force into two parts – tradesmen, who were mainly Protestant, and labourers, who were mainly Catholic. It provided a major advantage for the employers in that it enabled them to subordinate all workers' interests on the shop floor to those of their own.

Forced upon the Catholic citizens at a time when they were suffering multiple deprivation of a social and economic character, this ideology brought conflict and serious rioting on to the streets of Belfast. A similar pattern of events faced American blacks at the beginning of the 1960s when they were forced to come north to look for subsistence. Like the nineteenth-century Catholics in Belfast, they found poor housing in ghetto areas, low-paid jobs and unemployment, in addition to a social control mechanism that encompassed their occupations, their churches, their culture, their ethics and their relationship with law enforcement agencies.[5]

The Unionist Government, which had evolved its political strategy over a long period, exercised equally gross forms of discrimination against Catholics in support of that strategy.

As a result of this long-established and consistently applied tactic, rioting between Catholic and Protestant inhabitants of Belfast commenced sometime in the 1830s. Then it was usually of the sporadic type that seldom carried over to a second day, but from 1852 onwards it took a turn for the worse: house-wrecking and shootings were added to prolonged stoning – all of which appeared to have an element of co-ordination.

The consequence of this more vicious rioting was the large-scale evacuation of families from houses in mixed religious areas. The evacuees were mainly those of the Catholic faith and they were forced to move back into their own homogeneous areas in Belfast or to emigrate to the south of Ireland for safety. This contained advantages for the bourgeoisie as well as for the Protestant craftsmen who were feeling more threatened at this time by the increasing numbers of Catholic labourers coming to Belfast. The threat of an unengaged labour force, prepared to take employment in Belfast factories and shipyards at low wages, could be used to keep down labour costs. When a bourgeois political organisation was established around the 1860s it contrived to create the same basic conflicts to ensure Orange support against the danger of the Catholic voter in their midst.

This attempt to organise the skilled workers in Belfast into a political force coincided with the Liberals' efforts to draw support from skilled workers in Britain after the introduction of the Reform Act in 1867. To some extent, the attempt by the Belfast bourgeoisie represented the first groping steps towards a ruling-class control of Belfast workers both economically and politically. By the time the Home Rule Bill of 1886 was being debated in the House of Commons the Unionists had organised themselves into a coherent movement and were now concentrating their efforts on the political front.

Elections, henceforth, were foregone conclusions because the majority vote, consisting of the Protestant skilled workers, as against the minority vote, consisting of unskilled and unemployed workers, made the Unionists electorally invincible. Nevertheless rioting remained an important element in the Unionist policy of containing the growth of the Catholic minority in the population of Belfast.

One incident which arose out of a march on 15 August 1864 is illustrative of this. On a Catholic feast day, 400 Catholic navvies building a graving dock in the Belfast Harbour marched to Brown Square, a Protestant stronghold. The navvies went there to avenge earlier attacks on Catholic areas by Protestant workers but were driven off by foundry workers after attacking a local school. The following day, shipyard workers, responding to the news of the navvies' attack on the school, marched to the centre of Belfast and plundered gunsmiths and hardware merchants of weapons. On the succeeding morning, armed with their deadly weapons, 600 shipwrights descended on the Catholic navvies who were at work at the docks and drove them into the sloblands of the Harbour Estate.[6]

This attack was the start of large-scale rioting which lasted for a number of weeks and led ultimately to the reorganisation of the police in Belfast. Eleven people were killed, 300 injured and 100 suffered gunshot wounds.

Below is part of an Orange ballad, written by an unknown shipyard carpenter and part of the Aiken McClelland Collection, called 'The Battle of the Navvies'.

The navvies fought like bulldogs but we swore to put them down –
The assassins of the children, the despoilers of the town!
Some struggle in the deadly gripe, some load away and fire;
Ho! Ho! the navvies show their backs and down the bank retire,
Some leap into the river, some are scrambling through the mud,
And our noble fellows follow to the margin of the flood![7]

To some extent all rioting in Belfast afterwards was instigated by forces in the shipyard even though the explicit causes may have emanated from other sources.

From 1852 onwards, rioting was reported to have broken out on average once every seven years. One consequence of the constant rioting was that the population of Belfast polarised almost completely along religious lines. Each section of the community moved towards its own areas for security. Jobs in factories in these areas would invariably go to those who lived nearest. There were few factories apart from low-wage linen mills in the Catholic areas, though when the trade cycle was favourable there was an abundance of well-paid jobs for skilled workers in Protestant areas.

When the trade cycle was unfavourable those few Catholics with jobs lost them and were forced to look for relief, provision of which was always inadequate. This was a deliberate policy of the Belfast Poor Law Guardians to prevent excessive immigration from the south and west of Ireland and to compel the unemployed to leave Belfast. The Guardians (mainly Protestant) did not provide relief to the city's destitute on the scale that was provided in other major cities in Great Britain. A comparison with Glasgow (which had the same social and economic structure) showed that 80 people per 1000 in Glasgow received relief as against 7 people per 1000 in Belfast.

The Catholic areas of Falls and Smithfield were also deprived of local authority representation until Westminster forced the Belfast City Council to recognise them as wards in the Boundary Extension Bill of 1896. Clear evidence of religious segregation was shown when new boundaries for local government elections were prepared after 1896. Fifteen new wards were created.

Table 4
Distribution and segregation of Roman Catholics in Belfast's electoral wards

WARD	1901	1911	INDEX 1926	1937	1951
Clifton	.86	.93	1.10	1.28	1.31
Court	.76	.96	.99	1.04	1.08
Cromac	.90	.90	.85	.93	.92
Dock	1.49	1.61	1.77	1.92	1.94
Duncairn	.71	.72	. 43	.44	.51
Falls	3.17	3.40	3.58	3.88	3.59
Ormeau	.57	.60	.30	.35	.38
Pottinger	.73	.70	.63	.59	.56
St. Anne's	1.43	1.39	1.68	1.59	1.57
St. George's	.40	.39	.20	.18	.17
Shankill	.31	.29	.19	.21	.25
Smithfield	3.58	3.68	3.95	3.86	3.52
Victoria	.39	.35	.24	.20	.25
Windsor	.62	.61	.72	.64	.60
Woodvale	.44	.41	.21	.19	.31

This table is based on a study by Emrys Jones in *Sociological Review*, IV, 1956.[8] Figures are a percentage of the overall population of Northern Ireland.

The table shows the number of Catholics living in each ward over a fifty-year span. In those wards where Catholics were in a majority or substantially entrenched, their numbers increased against a fall in the overall city population. Where they were in a minority their numbers continued to decline. In Falls, Smithfield, Dock and, to a lesser extent, Clifton, Court and St. Anne's wards, a slight rise was recorded. Decreases were recorded in the other wards where Catholics were substantially in the minority.

Catholics were forced to live in poverty from the first. They had arrived in Belfast from the most poverty-stricken parts of Ireland; some to escape the hunger and agony of the famine and others to find

21

work and relief from the constant distress and misery of their home-
lands.

In the late nineteenth century Rev. W.M. O'Hanlon described
living conditions in Smithfield, one of the main Catholic areas, as
'dangerous and perishing... classes trying to exist amidst scenes of
strident poverty.'[9] At the same time one out of every two inmates of
the Belfast workhouses was a Catholic even though less than one out of
every four Belfast citizens was of that faith. The same was still true at
the turn of the century when accurate figures were collected for the
Census of Ireland Returns for 1901.

O'Hanlon had selected a number of houses as being representative
of the squalor and wretchedness of the area. He found families,
sometimes as many as seven persons, living in a single room of each
house, using straw on the floor as bedding. The windows had no glass
and were open to the extremes of the weather. The inhabitants had
little food to eat and were forced to huddle together to keep themselves warm. The men were unskilled and were unemployed for long
periods. The women and girls who were able to do so worked at home
sewing muslin which they had to collect and return in large bundles to
the linen warehouses. They were paid at the rate of sevenpence or
eightpence a week. Full-time workers in the factories earned one
shilling and sixpence a week and skilled workers from four shillings to
six shillings when the market for linen products was thriving.[10]

Figures recorded that in 1901 40 per cent of bare-footed spinners, 29
per cent of weavers, 41 per cent of dockers, 13 per cent of commercial
clerks, 8 per cent of municipal clerks and 7 per cent of shipwrights,
were Catholics.

The figures not only reflected that the Catholics occupied the
lowest-paid jobs but also implied that Orange political influence on
public boards in employment recruitment policy was all-important in
the selection for these positions.

An earlier example of this is to be found in the Census of Ireland
1891, in which Catholics are recorded as representing 26.3 per cent of
the population of Belfast. A Select Committee Report for the House
of Commons 1892 shows in its minutes covering the same period that
the following position obtained:

	Protestants	Catholics
Belfast Corporation:		
Members	40	0
Paid Staff	89	2
Belfast Harbour Board:		
Members	22	0
Paid Staff	37	0
Water Commissioners:		
Members	15	1
Paid Staff	7	0
Poor Law Board:	43	1
Paid Staff	91	3
	350	**7**

Protestant Total 350 (98%)
Catholic Total   7 (2%)

Giving evidence later, before the same Select Committee on the Belfast Corporation Bill 1896, the Lord Mayor of Belfast, Mr W.J. Pirrie, admitted that an annual expenditure of £144,000 was paid out to Belfast contractors, none of whom was Catholic. It was noted that about £40,000 was paid in salaries to officials employed by the Belfast Corporation, Belfast Harbour Board, Belfast Poor Law Board and the Water Commission – only 1¼ per cent went to Catholic employees.[11].

Catholics were also less than proportionately represented in skilled jobs, in the professions and in middle-class employment but over-represented in unskilled jobs and in domestic services.[12] Returns for 1901 state that out of every ten skilled workers in engineering one was a Catholic; one out of every twelve merchants and one out of every thirteen lawyers were Catholic; but that one out of every two employed in low-paid labouring jobs was a Catholic. Inherent in the employment problem was the fact that ownership of industry, apart from a few Catholic traders in the depth of their own ghetto, was exclusively in the hands of Protestants. Therefore the selection of the 'right' people for employment in the private sector of the economy, aided and abetted by the early craft unions, was consistent with the political needs of the Unionist establishment.

The Unionist Party, as formed in the 1860s, grew out of an amalgamation of the Orange Order and Belfast Conservatives. It had existed earlier under several other names as a political force formed mainly to resist the O'Connell-led Repeal Movement. From its establishment however its chief activities were organised towards resisting the growth of the Catholic population, consolidating its own power and putting a stop to Gladstone's Home Rule Bill.

The new party from the start actively encouraged rioting by their supporters to compel Belfast Catholics to leave and deter others from the south of Ireland from coming to replace them. No such deterrent was placed before Protestants coming from the same areas: indeed, they were absorbed with exaggerated affection into the Belfast community.

Belfast's economic expansion had been extraordinary by any standards. When it commenced early in the nineteenth century a large reserve of labour was required by entrepreneurs. Once the movement of the workers and their families started towards Belfast it was not possible to regulate it to meet the vagaries of the Belfast trade cycle. Those Belfast institutions and agencies which were obliged to provide relief for the newcomers in times of hardship neglected to do so under political prompting. At times when the trade volume subsided, traditional fears and suspicions were aroused by the bourgeoisie and exploded into violence which was savage and sustained. As firearms became easy to obtain, death tolls mounted.

The worst sectarian trouble, however, came in 1920, after the establishment of the new Parliament in Stormont, with a pogrom against Catholic families. Newspapers reports of July 1920 are filled with stories of Catholics fighting hand-to-hand to defend their homes and families against overwhelming odds. Some were overpowered and killed in full view of their children. Over 450 people were shot dead: 270 Catholics and 185 Protestants, while more than 2,000 were wounded. Rioting mobs caused £3 million damage in Catholic areas.

The Belfast bourgeoisie thus had developed a strategy that not only had the effect of curtailing the number of Catholic immigrants to Belfast but also created the power base for entrepreneurs whose lineal descendants form the Unionist hegemony of the twentieth century. It was the tactics adopted by entrepreneurs in the nineteenth century which led to the events set out in the following chapters.

3
Early Trade Unions in Belfast

Trade unionism in Belfast was concentrated in the shipbuilding and engineering factories in the immediate area of the Belfast Harbour Estate and beyond. Little traces of it were found elsewhere except where tiny pockets of workers belonging to the old craft unions or guilds practised their skills. These workers pursued their trades in the small shops that abound in the narrow streets around the River Farset on which Belfast was built.

By 1811 however the great Cotton Operatives' Union, which had membership throughout Britain, was reported to have a branch in Belfast.

Not only were the weavers of Belfast organised in the Union but also those in the country around the Maze district of Lisburn. In April 1815 a large number of these workers were reported to have marched into Belfast, leaving their webs unwoven at the warerooms as a protest against reduced wages. When the magistrates attempted to arrest the leaders rioting broke out. The most serious outrage took place in February 1816 when some twenty men attempted to blow up the house of an unpopular manufacturer in Belfast. Two men who had been found guilty of taking part were hanged in Belfast in September. In April 1817 Gordon Maxwell of Lisburn, the President of the Muslin Weavers' Society, was fatally wounded on the Malone Road. Before his death he accused his employer, John McCann, of the crime. McCann was put on trial for his life but acquitted. In 1818 there was another serious strike although conditions had somewhat improved after the incidents of 1817.

The Rev. William O'Hanlon relates the story of five Belfast tailors combining to request an increase in wages. They were promptly arrested, tried by the town magistrate and sent to jail – all on the one day!

These weavers worked from their own homes on material given out for processing and which was returned, when finished, to the owner's warehouse. Once Belfast was caught up in the Industrial Revolution, workers who had worked at home at their own pace were collected into factories and forced to labour there with mechanical frequency. Ties with the old trade unions were weakened and soon disappeared. A fresh element however began to obstruct the combination of workers in their attempts to improve their wages and conditions in these new working arrangements – the friction between the original town-dwellers who were Protestant by religion and the later arrivals who were Catholics. This friction was exploited by the Belfast employers. Alexander Moncrieff, a manufacturer, was quoted in 1835 as saying that Scottish capitalists were coming to Belfast where they found labour cheaper since the differences between Catholic and Orange weavers kept them from combining in trade unions.[1]

Moncrieff's point about workers failing for religious reasons to combine was confirmed six years later when the weavers of east Belfast went on strike to protest against the high price of food, only to be accused by their own leaders of selling 'the Orange cause for the big loaf'. The Sovereign of Belfast banned the protest, and the strikers, in the face of total opposition from the Orangemen and the bourgeoisie of Belfast were forced back to work.

Trade unionism in Belfast differed from that in any similar city in the United Kingdom as it was inextricably tied to the Orange Order in its daily activities.

Formed in the 1780s to defend the Protestant religion, the Order had lodges for workers, foremen, managers and owners of factories. As a consequence it had more power and authority, and drew more loyalty from the workers than any trade union. In the early days of trade unions it was the Orange Order's Worshipful Masters on the shop floor who had real power and who represented the worker when he had reason to complain or to seek better working conditions from his bosses.

As the Belfast trade volume increased, unions for skilled workers were established. These unions retained their links with the Orange Order and were always influenced by the city's bourgeoisie. All that was needed was the opportunity to convert the arrangement into a political strategy. The Home Rule question proved to be one such opportunity. The evolution of this strategy and its subsequent development is basic to this study of how the Poor Law was used against a section of Northern Ireland society for political purposes, and why, moreover, an important institution such as the trade union movement had little or no role in securing social justice, as it was morally obliged to do, for a substantial segment of its members.

There were formidable obstacles to overcome before the predominately female flax and textile workers could form themselves into a trade union. First of all, mills and factories in Belfast were owned by Protestants. As long as the workers were part of religious ghettoes whose inhabitants were deeply hostile to one another, it was never possible to secure the pre-requisite solidarity and goodwill for them to unite on a factory or industrial basis to help themselves against their employers. Also, the mill-owners owned the adjacent houses in which the workers and their families lived.

Workers joining a trade union against their employers' wishes would be summarily dismissed and would lose their homes as a consequence. Although the textile workers believed that by joining a trade union improvements to wages and conditions would follow, their husbands and families often disapproved of their independence in wanting to join a trade union. It suggested behaviour unbecoming a respectable woman in a Protestant society like Belfast. Nevertheless, towards the end of the century firm efforts were made by Mary Galway of the Textile Operatives Society of Ireland, and later by James Connolly of the Irish Transport and General Workers' Union, to organise these workers. Their efforts had no lasting effect. Indeed, I recall, as recently as 1938, listening to trade union leaders trying to convince workers as they hurried into mills on the Falls Road of the benefits of being in a union. They had no success until recent years, by which time the industry was badly blighted.

Trade unions did exist, of course, in Belfast in the nineteenth century, but some of them took odd forms. The few that are relevant to this book were located in the shipyard and engineering factories in Belfast. The first reference to one of these was in 1843 when the iron shipyard opened in Belfast and the skilled workers formed a trade union with the title of 'Belfast Protestant Operatives' Society'.[2] This Society was formed at a time when the Protestant majority felt the need for some arrangements in employment which would protect their economic interests against further incursion of Catholics.

There is evidence to show that pressure from Protestant skilled workers was applied to keep Catholics from being recruited into the shipyard. Certainly the Orange Order put pressure on local foremen, members of the Order who had authority to 'start and stop' labour, not to employ Catholics. Evidence is still available from registers of trade unions which were formed later to show that few Catholics were employed as skilled workers. This form of screening of workers for religious reasons applied to practically every engineering establishment in the Belfast area from the time that the iron shipyard was established. (Later, when the Belfast Protestant Operatives' Society foundered, the Orange Order's organisation on the shop floor still continued its strictures on Catholic recruitment until the present craft unions took over that function again.)

Adults who were skilled at their trades had to be spoken for by safe Orangemen before being taken on by sympathetic managements. Apprentices, who constituted the main force of recruits, were introduced by Orangemen to the management. They also had to sign an agreement to pay the employer an indemnity before being engaged as an indentured apprentice – a further barrier, this time financial. Thus entry to the entire range of engineering trades could be controlled. The system of recruitment, as far as Orangemen were concerned, was foolproof. Only those well disposed towards Orangeism were employed in the iron and steel industries. Those not so disposed found themselves jobs elsewhere, as labourers, assisting the hewers of wood, and drawers of water, or else remaining unemployed.

When trade union organisation took a more structured form in the late nineteenth century, control of the emerging craft unions was still in the hands of the Orange Order. Skilled workers came to see themselves as 'the aristocracy of labour'.[3] They were conscious of their superiority over unskilled fellow-workers and of living in neighbourhoods of a higher social status. They believed, in addition, that they had a common interest with their employers in matters of education and welfare, in social and cultural affiliations, and in politics. Long apprenticeships, developed skills, respectability and membership of certain Orange Lodges which had an aura of exclusiveness, reinforced their belief in their privileged position in Belfast society. This feeling existed throughout British industry as well, but to a lesser extent in factories where skilled workers were concentrated in large production units. Amongst the skilled workers of Belfast, however, the feeling was heavily buttressed by the strength of religious hostility to the unskilled and unemployed workers.

Relations between the Belfast craft unions and their employers were entirely different from those in the United Kingdom. In other cities there was natural conflict between them on issues like human rights, wages, working conditions and lay-offs. In Belfast the same issues existed but in lower tones and the natural conflict was replaced by a willingness on the part of these interests to accommodate one another for reasons that were not always explicit. With the myth that the entire community was 'under siege', the employers and employees of Belfast could see it a common duty to try to merge their industrial interests as well as their political identities so that shop-floor differences would not place the security of the community at risk.

The skilled workers were fair game for the prejudices of the bourgeoisie, particularly after the Home Rule issue arose in 1886 when they were persuaded that they had a moral role to play in defending the Protestant 'ethic'. The matter of collaboration, therefore, between capital and labour, skilled workers and employer, Orange voter and Unionist politician, is easily explained. For years the labourers in Belfast had toiled, ignored by the better-off skilled workers alongside them, on miserable wages and working conditions. Unlike labourers in engineering shops in major cities across the water, who had been helped to form their own unions by craft union leaders like Tom Mann, John Burns and Ben Tillett, labourers in Belfast prior to 1907 were offered by their craft union brethren neither membership of a common union nor assistance to form their own combinations to improve their working existence.

Unskilled workers at the docks were singularly unsuccessful in forming a trade union. In 1889 the National Union of Dock Labourers (NUDL) operated a branch for dockers for a short time. Several other efforts to organise the dock workers were made but there was little interest shown by the dockers when those unions that did exist were seen to be controlled by the owner's nominees.[4]

Apart from the NUDL efforts to form a branch, several other unions, catering generally for unskilled workers, were organised from time to time in Belfast. These were the Municipal Employees' Association which had ties with Will Thorne's Gasworkers in London, the National Amalgamated Union of Labour (NAUL) and the Textile Operatives Society of Ireland. These last two merged some years later into the Amalgamated Transport and General Workers' Union. These unions were subjected to persecution in the early years of the century by the Belfast employers who refused to meet them on their members' behalf on any matter concerning wages or conditions of work. On one occasion in 1907 unskilled workers employed by Sirocco Works went on strike on the simple issue of trying to force management 'into meeting their union representative. The official, Mr George Greig of the NAUL recounted his efforts to secure an interview with their employer.

Had Mr. Davidson [the employer] treated me or his men with one half of the courtesy that he shows to representatives of skilled workmen, his works need not have stood idle for a day. The fact remains that those who have been well enough organised to enforce fair treatment have got it, while those who have not been organised are, if the firm can prevent it, not to be allowed to become members of a trade union.[5]

Since 1906 all unskilled workers in Sirocco Works had been required to sign an undertaking that they would not be members of any labourers' society or union while employed by the firm.

The following year when the NAUL called the labourers out on strike for a wage increase, Samuel C. Davidson, the managing director, dismissed them. A statement which he issued to the press was revealing:

One hundred and twenty of the men who have been on strike have agreed to resume work on the Company's terms so that at any moment we can go full steam ahead... we had had a sort of spring cleaning and when the dust is shaken out of the carpets, the microbes will not come back.

In 1913 the prohibition against union membership for unskilled workers became more specific with the lockout of similar workers by their employers in Dublin.

Davidson, like William Martin Murphy who was responsible for the Dublin lockout, forced unskilled workers to sign a declaration that they were not to be members of the Irish Transport and General Workers' Union (ITGWU) or any other unskilled labourers' society and that they would not join or become members in the future.[6]

For a number of years prior to this, craft unions in the engineering and shipbuilding industries had been recognised by the Belfast employers. Wage rates were determined in England and applied to all United Kingdom regions, including Belfast. Unskilled workers in the same industries in Belfast were kept outside the scope of the wage agreements. Attempts made to organise labourers into a union were met with hostility from the employers and indifference from the craft unions. In 1893 unionised platers in the Shipyard disgraced themselves by using blacklegs to cut their helpers' wages during a six weeks' strike. The wages were below the English level and platers' helpers successfully resisted the cuts.[7]

An organisation called the Employers' Protestant Association defined the employers' attitude to trade unions they wished to favour as against those they did not:

> Trade unions, as the name itself implies, are associations or societies of tradesmen who have been skilled artizans, by each man having had to serve an apprenticeship of generally five years, and at most trades working as an improver for another two years, making a total of seven years before being entitled to rank of a journeyman. The equality of apprenticeship constitutes a reasonable basis for the unions of each individual trade to claim equal minimum wages for each of their fully-qualified tradesmen. Labour unions, on the other hand, are organised societies of unskilled workers, the only qualification for membership being the payment of an entrance fee and of a small weekly contribution. Apprenticeship, which is the primary qualification of trade unions and the only sound foundation on which a minimum rate of wages can be based, is therefore totally absent in labour unions.
>
> It would be unreasonable to expect that an absolutely inexperienced labouring man would, by merely joining a union, thereby become entitled to the pay of the most experienced as it would be for the youngest apprentice to a trade to be entitled to a journeyman's minimum wage, from the very day he started his apprenticeship.[8]

The employers' case against labouring unions was as disingenuous as their opposition was unyielding. They pointed out in the same statement that to apply a labour union to every branch of business in Belfast would cause thorough disorganisation. Certainly the owners of Sirocco Engineering Works, always to the fore in these matters, thought this. When 300 unskilled workers sought to join a labouring union (their skilled workers had been members of a craft union for years) the owners threatened to move the entire plant to Germany.

The employers' serenity was disturbed in January 1907 when a union organiser from Liverpool called Jim Larkin arrived in the Belfast docklands on an organisational mission for the National Union of

Dock Labourers. Larkin's efforts at organising the docks met with overwhelming success. By April he had recruited 3,000 employees of the largest coal importer in Belfast, John Kelly & Co. The employers then dismissed a number of men for refusing to leave the union. After a short, sharp skirmish, Kelly's conceded recognition and a general increase in wages to their workers.

Meanwhile, the Belfast Steamship Company had its own plans to deal with the issue of union recognition. When men knocked off work after refusing to work with non-union labour, the firm brought in fifty blacklegs from Liverpool to unload a ship. Immediately the whole labour force, all members of the NUDL, struck.

The strike was extremely violent and spread rapidly amongst the workers who handled cargo going out of and coming into the Port of Belfast. Moreover, it caught the attention and stirred the emotions of workers throughout Belfast. Long hours, low wages and the hard physical work which the carters and dockers had to do brought public sympathy to their side. Employers imported hundreds of blacklegs from England to fill the jobs of the strikers. They were attacked at every point. Ships coming through the narrow channel into the Belfast docks with blacklegs on board were attacked with missiles of all types. Pitched battles were fought daily as strikers fought to get at the blacklegs. Occasionally, they broke through and the blacklegs who were caught swore never to return to Belfast.

The behaviour of the employers and the authorities brought sympathy from the police to the strikers. This became manifest when Constable Barrett of the Royal Irish Constabulary was suspended for refusing to ride on a vehicle driven by a blackleg. Three hundred RIC men attempted to hold a meeting in Musgrave Street Station in the centre of Belfast but were stopped when Acting Commissioner Morrell intervened. He was knocked to the floor for his troubles. A number of policemen were dismissed as a result, including Barrett, and most of the others were transferred from Belfast immediately afterwards.[9]

After this incident the military were called in to take over peace-keeping duties although the police had never abandoned their responsibility for law and order. This decision was controversial. Hostility had always existed between the Catholics in the Falls Road area and the military and it was assumed that once the army became involved the prospect of confining the trouble to industrial areas would disappear. The employers had been pressing for their use because the police appeared to favour the strikers and police powers, as applied in the strike, had not been repressive enough to drive the strikers back to work. The military, on the other hand, were assumed to have the freedom they needed to engage in an all-out war against the strikers.

The employers had been at their wits' end to find some means of breaking the solidarity of the workers. Indeed, the master carriers had spent the initial three hours of one meeting discussing the best way to raise the Home Rule issue which they believed would turn one section of the strikers against the other on a sectarian basis.

The employers, however, had a turn of good fortune when, on 11 August 1907, two drunks were arrested after a brawl in a street off the Falls Road. The van taking them to police headquarters was attacked by a mob; reinforcements were sent for and within a few hours the Falls area was a scene of serious rioting.

Strike leaders arrived in the area to appeal for peace but their pleas went unheeded. Knowing that if the trouble got out of hand the strike could be lost, they moved strikers into the area carrying placards asking the residents not to be misled. The Belfast Trades Council issued a statement showing what their game was:

> The employers of Belfast and the Authorities are trying to make the present disturbance a party matter for they know that if they can get Protestants and Catholics to fight one another they can beat the workers. This is not a fight between Protestant and Catholic but between the employers, backed by the authorities, and the workers. Not as Catholic and Protestant, as Nationalist or Unionist, but as Belfast men and workers, stand together and don't be misled by the employers' game of dividing us.

Nevertheless, the rioting continued and the following day a detachment of 100 troops was sent by the Lord Mayor to occupy the Model School on the Falls Road. At 5.55 pm Major Thackeray, a local magistrate, accompanied the soldiers and quickly read the Riot Act from the steps of the school to passers-by who were going about their business in peace. Within the hour two young people coming from work were shot dead.

Reports of the shooting worsened the situation. Casualties were heavy on both sides. Many arrests were made. The Custody Court was kept open throughout the night. The combined police and military operation was having no effect and further shootings were feared. The following morning clergy and trade union leaders prevailed upon the

Lord Mayor to have the military withdrawn. After the inquest on the death of the two youths Major Thackerey was charged with manslaughter. The evidence given against him was that he ordered his troops to fire on a main road while the rioting was taking place in side streets. More evidence had been given that the two people shot in the back had been walking towards their homes from their places of work and that no proper warning had been given by the military before firing.

If the military intervention was a pre-arranged plot by the bourgeoisie to divert public attention from the strike, as was suspected by trade unionists, then it worked, but it failed lamentably to have any effect on the solidarity of the strikers. That solidarity, though under severe pressure, held against the strain. Trade union pickets were organised immediately and sent to areas around the Falls to ensure that the peace was kept while the strike lasted.

Several months afterwards a series of conferences was held in Belfast and the employers conceded something on almost every issue. The union had won the right at last to represent its members with every company trading in Belfast Harbour. But the saga had not ended with the recognitions of the union; the bourgeoisie of Belfast and their supporters were not easily brushed to the side. On 26 October, some weeks after the return to work, several companies offered work to men who claimed that they were members of the Belfast Coalworkers' and Carters' Benefit Society. Information was received spontaneously by the NUDL that the Society was established to cater for Protestants only. Work stopped on every vessel that had reported activity by members of the new Society. The employers claimed that under the new agreement they had the right to employ whomsoever they chose. With that, they immediately started to recruit non-union labour but the cranemen refused to work with them. Dockers in Newry and Derry struck in sympathy with the Belfast dockers.

It was plain to see that the Orange Order had intervened on behalf of the employers by arranging non-union Protestant labour. It was a stealthy manoeuvre aimed at breaking the hard-forged solidarity of the labouring men at the docks. But the Orange Order's intervention failed. Larkin was reported afterwards in the Belfast Trades Council records as blaming the Boilermakers' Union for having set up the new Society to serve the interests of the employers at the instigation of the Orangemen. He repeated this allegation on a number of occasions and was never really rebutted by the Boilermakers' Union – one of whose leading members was president of the Belfast Trades Council.

Prior to the 1907 strike the Belfast Trades Council reflected the views of craft unions which were mainly expressed in narrow conservative terms by the skilled union delegates who attended the monthly meetings. On one occasion, in 1894, the President, a printer, and the Vice-President, an iron founder, resigned their positions partly because they considered that labourers were over-represented on the council. Few Catholics presented themselves as delegates until the labouring unions affiliated after 1907 and little value was attached to the small contribution they made to debates because of their lack of experience and support. Representation from the skilled unions was 90 per cent of the membership of the Trades Council. It was heavily consolidated because of the constant immigration from shipbuilding areas like Glasgow and Liverpool.

Billie McMullan, former President of the Irish Transport and General Workers' Union, described representatives to the Council as being steeped in the orthodox trade union tradition of Belfast and full of sectarian prejudice. They certainly seemed a pompous lot with an exaggerated estimation of their importance to Belfast. On one occasion they took it upon themselves to warn the working men of Belfast about Keir Hardie, who at that time was to speak at an Independent Labour meeting, urging them 'to take no notice of irresponsible parties who are endeavouring to propound their ideas under the mantle of Trade Unionism and Labour'.

William Walker, the President of the Council for a number of years, expressed the opinion that he represented the desire of the Unionist worker to combine the constitutional views of the Ulster Unionist Council with the social politics of the British Labour Party. There can be little doubt that he did reflect the opinions of the craft union delegates, with several notable exceptions. In later years he was nominated and supported by the Trades Council on three separate occasions in Westminster elections – all of which he lost to Unionist candidates.

Perhaps the distinction between the Belfast Trades Council and those of the other major cities in Britain is best marked by an event that happened in a 1905 by-election in which Walker was the trade union and labour candidate. During the days of the election preparation, Walker was approached by the Secretary of the Belfast Protestant Association to answer thirteen questions that were designed to determine his attitude to the Protestant Ascendancy. In the course of his reply he stated that he would fight to retain the British Sovereign's Accession Declaration against transubstantiation which describes the 'sacrifice of the Mass as superstitious and idolatrous'; that he would work to exclude Catholics from the high offices of Lord High Chancellor and Lord Lieutenant of Ireland. He added, quite unnecessarily, in the interview which followed, that 'Protestantism means protesting against superstition, hence true Protestantism is synonymous with Labour'. When Ramsay McDonald, who was acting as election agent, heard of the interview he wanted to resign and return to London by the next boat. He was persuaded not to do so because of the effect his leaving would have on the labour movement in Belfast. Walker was narrowly defeated by Sir Daniel Dixon who had the wisdom not to reply to such ridiculous questions.[10]

Walker was applauded by his Trades Council colleagues at their next meeting for his outstanding performance by being beaten only by the slender margin of 510 votes. No reference was made in the minutes to Walker's replies to the Belfast Protestant Association. It must be presumed that the delegates were not offended as was Ramsay McDonald by this public display of anti-Catholicism.

After a period of comparative calm after the social reforms of the Liberal Government the Trades Council was devastated from 1912 onwards by the events which accompanied the Home Rule debates at Westminster. Many Catholics lost their jobs and both the trade union movement and the budding Labour Party were driven underground in the hysteria which followed the Home Rule Act going on the Statute Book.

World War One however, brought a change of climate and the Trades Council as well as the Labour Party came again to the forefront when the working-class movement took a leftward swing in 1919.

4

The Setting-Up of the Northern Ireland Regime

On 22 December 1919 the British Government announced that it intended to establish two Parliaments in Ireland which would administer, on the one hand, six of the nine Ulster counties, and, on the other, the rest of Ireland. It was the intention of the Government that each proposed Parliament would have only a limited set of powers, with extra provisions enshrined in the Government of Ireland Act to enable them to amalgamate later by mutual agreement.

The structure of government for Northern Ireland was poorly conceived; a temporary arrangement which the British Government devised to get around the constitutional difficulties of setting up the Free State. Little real power was transferred to the new Government though it did receive authority for local affairs, trade, industry, education, agriculture, social services, and law and order. Westminster, however, was still to be the sovereign power and all Acts passed there were to extend automatically to Northern Ireland unless specifically excluded by amendment.

The announcement of a settlement was the culmination of a long period of unrest in Ireland which had been triggered during the previous generation by repeated controversies over a Home Rule Bill for Ireland. Among the many fierce controversies that arose as a result of this announcement, one directly relevant to this book concerned the nature of the administration that was to be formed by Ulster politicians. During the passage of the Bill at Westminster to set up the new regime, the intransigence of the Ulster Unionist leaders was robustly expressed. Fears for the future of Catholics living there were heightened by the bitter speeches being made by the Ulster MPs.

That concern was the main theme of King George V's speech on the opening of the Northern Ireland Parliament in June 1921, when he stated that he prayed his coming to Ireland would be the first step towards the end of strife amongst Irish people whatever their race or creed.[1]

His sentiments were the antithesis of those expressed by the local Unionist leaders on the same occasion. They made no bones about it being a 'Protestant Parliament for a Protestant people'. Certainly James Craig expressed this sentiment on a number of occasions – so often indeed that the King's speech was assumed to have been made to mitigate the effects of Craig's speeches on other Commonwealth countries.

The die was cast by the tone and temper of speeches made by Sir Edward Carson and the politician who was later to become the first Prime Minister of Northern Ireland. Mr James Craig, MP, choosing to ignore the claims of the other Ulster counties, Cavan, Monaghan and Donegal, for inclusion in the new statelet, said on 10 March 1920 at Westminster:

> If we had a nine-county Parliament with sixty four members the Unionist majority would be three or four, but in a six-county Parliament with fifty-two members, the Unionist majority would be about ten. We would frankly admit that we cannot hold the nine counties. The three included counties containing 70,000 Unionists to 200,000 Sinn Feiners and Nationalists and the addition of that large block of Sinn Feiners and Nationalists would reduce our majority to such a level that no sane man would undertake to carry on a Parliament with it.

However, Craig could see further difficulties even after he was able to divest his Parliament of the three Ulster counties with anti-Unionist majorities. He feared that the higher Catholic birth rate would rapidly turn a minority into a majority. This fear was to determine both Craig's and Unionists' policies throughout the period covered by this study. The strategy which evolved and had been applied on an ad-hoc basis prior to 1920, became woven into the policy of each government department.

Catholics were to be excluded from most government departments and, where it was possible to use influence, from private employment. This was to force them on to public relief, which would be refused or reduced thereby forcing them to transfer their families to the south of Ireland for the means to exist.

However, there were other difficulties to overcome. For example, the Unionist strategy for keeping political control would have to depend on the Government's ability to keep issues on strict sectarian lines – loyalty to the religious and political symbols of the Party. If the Government got over that difficulty they could keep their party in power indefinitely. Therefore, they had to get adequate necessities of life to their own supporters, while at the same time depriving the others who did not support the new state of these same necessities.

The way the Government set out to achieve this was by setting up a screening arrangement which enabled only their supporters to get jobs and unemployment insurance payments. Others would receive nothing, or no more than a pittance for relief.

This task was made easy for them by the trend begun in the previous century, when skilled workers, under bourgeoisie promptings, became supporters of the Belfast establishment while the labourers, who were mainly Catholic, did not.

The next phase of the Government of Ireland Act was the drawing up of the boundaries for Northern Ireland. Southern Ireland representatives on the Boundary Commission withdrew when it was seen by them that the draft report would draw conclusions favouring the Northern Unionists. Implicit in that report was the necessity for the Unionists to maximise the influence of 820,000 Unionists and minimise that of the 420,000 Nationalists. This the Unionists, who were elected to office in a landslide victory, set out to do by the transfer of institutions and agencies to their control. It was their belief that the Catholics, either Nationalists or Sinn Feiners, were disloyal to the British Crown, therefore to the Unionist Party, and had no right to participate in the running of the affairs of the state or to expect fair treatment from its institutions.

A settlement on these terms would give the Unionists perpetual domination of the North's political affairs. As long as politics in Northern Ireland were conducted on religious lines, the Unionists could not lose an election. The prerequisite for keeping this formula intact was that all political exchanges would range between two sets of Nationalists – British, who were Protestant, and Irish, who were Catholic. They believed that compromise or concessions to the minority would be fatal to their hegemony. Unionist ideology, therefore, was strictly imposed and token Catholic reaction to it cynically exploited. The position, now that the Unionists were in power, was radically different from that which obtained in the pre-partition era.

The setting-up of the state of Northern Ireland enabled the Unionists to institutionalise the violence they provoked earlier against the Catholic minority.

This could not have worked if the Belfast bourgeoisie had been faced by a militant trade union movement pushing forward for higher wages or a fairer share of wealth and profits. Class politics such as those that developed from 1919 in Great Britain, could have caused the Unionist downfall if the entire working class of Belfast had united in support of these issues. The Unionist strategy which had evolved over the years was pursued now more than ever to keep the workers apart by imposing on them issues that had little relation to their class interests. Instead they were ensnared by economic and social issues only slightly more sophisticated than those posed by the uncouth superstitious Catholic labourer of the 1880s. By this time, Catholics were presented to Unionist supporters as IRA gunmen acting at the Pope's behest to steal their jobs and their property.

Ramsay McDonald perceived this strategy in 1912 when he said at Westminster:

> In Belfast you get labour conditions the like of which you get in no other town, no other city of equal commercial prosperity from John O'Groats to Land's End or from the Atlantic to the North Sea. It is maintained by an exceedingly simple device... Whenever there is an attempt to root out sweating in Belfast the Orange big drum is beaten.[2]

The IRA proved to be a life-saver to the Unionist Government. If they had not been active the Unionists would have had to create an IRA to save themselves from the new working-class militancy which ex-soldiers brought back with them from France.

A Unionist historian describes the position as follows:

> After 1920 their objective was to maintain the Union. The strategy they employed was simple, short term and effective. They maintained themselves in power by banging the big drum, waving the flag and playing upon the emotions of the Protestant population.[3]

It followed that thereafter politics in Northern Ireland would be kept to sectarian or tribal lines and Catholics excluded from public employment whether in local government or in the civil service. Certainly there is evidence available to show that those Catholics who had been employed in Civil Service jobs were replaced by 'safe' people of the Protestant faith.

Heads of departments in the Civil Service in Dublin, who were responsible for establishing new Ministries in the North after the Treaty, were told bluntly by the new Government that no Catholics would be employed and to take them off the staff list for transfer to the North. This happened when Sir Edward Archdale, the new Minister of Agriculture, brought an Englishman over to run his department. He took this step to prevent an Irish Catholic, who was a senior civil servant in Dublin, from being transferred to Belfast to take the job. He was acutely embarrassed when it was discovered that the Englishman was a Catholic.[4]

Archdale's reaction to Catholic civil servants was not in isolation to that of his Cabinet colleagues. Dawson Bates, Minister of Home Affairs, was reported in 1923 as saying that he would not have a Catholic working in his Ministry as he would not trust his loyalty to the Government.[5] Indeed as late as 1934 he learned with shock that a Catholic telephonist had been engaged by the Ministry of Finance to work on the switchboard at Stormont buildings. He refused to use the telephone until she was removed.

John Andrews, Minister of Labour, was reported to have sacked two Catholics from his department when he returned from holiday in 1926.[6] Both Ministers were adamant that Catholics would not be employed in their departments because by their presence they could inhibit the working of the strategy.

Dame Enid Lyons, widow of Joseph A. Lyons, Catholic PM of Australia in the 1930s, recalls in her memoirs a famous gaffe illustrative of Craig's own feelings:

> It was Lord Craigavon, the fiercely anti-Catholic Prime Minister of Northern Ireland, who, knowing nothing of Joe's personal background, had asked him at a banquet in London, 'Lyons, have you got many Catholics in Australia?' 'Oh, about one in five,' Joe had replied. 'Well, watch 'em, Lyons, watch 'em,' Craigavon had urged. 'They breed like bloody rabbits.'[7]

Sir Wilfrid Spender, the Cabinet Secretary, wrote in his diary that he told the Cabinet in 1934 that no Catholics were to be found amongst the permanent or assistant secretaries of the civil service since he came into the post in 1925. No Catholics had entered the administrative ranks since then. There was a chart available for these ranks in 1927 which shows one permanent secretary and one assistant secretary described as Catholics. Presumably they were in post by 1925 and had left or were retired by 1934.

1927		Protestant %		Catholic %
Permanent Secretary	5	83	1	17
Second and Assistant Secretary	12	92	1	8
Principals	40	93	3	7
Deputy and Assistant Principals	66	96	3	4
Staff Officers	92	94	6	6
Total	215	94	14	6

Cabinet minutes reveal that some effort was made by Mr Hugh Pollock, Minister of Finance, and Sir Wilfrid Spender, Secretary of the NI Cabinet, to persuade the other Ministers in the late Thirties to recruit Catholics into the Civil Service. Their efforts bore little fruit.[8]

It followed that the police force too would be reconstructed to suit the Government's interests and to protest its new institutions. The new force was named the Royal Ulster Constabulary and restricted Catholic recruitment to a quota which corresponded to the numbers of the population. Three new auxiliary forces were established: 'A', 'B', and 'C' Specials. Catholics, although not specifically excluded, were seldom enrolled as membership was tended to be drawn from the anti-Catholic Orange Order.

These forces acted directly under the instructions of Sir Dawson Bates, Minister of Home Affairs. They were used mainly for political purposes and within the framework of a Special Powers Act which was introduced almost immediately on the Unionists' taking office. The Special Powers Act and the political police forces gave the Government enormous scope to apply repressive measures against those who they believed were 'threatening the state'. They used them decisively on two occasions against IRA suspects: first, in 1922 when they detained several hundred suspects for nearly three years; and second, from 1938 to 1945 when 850 persons were detained.[9]

The Act, which was renewed annually in Parliament up to 1933, was used on a number of occasions by the Minister of Home Affairs to contain activities occasionally organised by the unemployed against hunger and distress. This was the other front that was engaging the Unionists' attention. It was equally important to their survival – in fact many of them regarded it as their Achilles' heel.

The essence of the Unionist strategy was to contain the Catholic minority in the new state to manageable proportions for electoral purposes, while at the same time pressurising the Catholics into emigration. The Unionist rationale after they were elected to government office in 1921 was to give legitimacy to all forms of pressure on their opponents to comply with their strategic requirements. They recognised the need for having constant elections and this for two reasons: to keep Westminster from interfering with their running of Northern Ireland, and to form a constitutional Opposition in the hope that wider support would be created externally for its existence as a state.

Their conception of democratic elections fell short of fair standards, but it effectively returned them at each election with comfortable majorities.

General Elections in Northern Ireland: 1921–1949 (52 seats)

Date	Unionist	Independent Unionist	Labour	Nationalist & associates	Others
24 May 1921	40	0	0	12	0
28 April 1925	33	3	3	12	1
22 May 1929	37	3	1	11	0
30 Nov. 1933	36	2	2	11	0
9 Feb. 1938	39	3	1	9	0
14 June 1945	33	2	2	12	3
28 Feb. 1949	37	2	0	11	2

Source: Northern Ireland Electoral Records

The foregoing record of these elections, which shows the breakdown of seats on a party basis, also tells the story of Unionist reaction to the flow of election returns. In 1921 no Labour candidate was returned at the ballot box, even though they had received one vote out of every five recorded in Belfast in the local elections the year before. That amount would have been sufficient for several successes under proportional representation. The labour challenge was pre-empted by the violence of Orange mobs at that first election held on 22 May 1921. Newspapers reported that there was intensive savagery and intimidation throughout the Loyalist parts of the city. Revolvers, knives, sticks and stones were used by mobs supporting Unionist candidates against Labour agents and voters. Vehicles were smashed. Nineteen cases of serious injury were taken to hospital. Irish Nationalists and Labour supporters were prevented from recording votes. The authorities took no action throughout the day to protect Opposition supporters who attempted to vote. Mr William Grant, a leader of the Ulster Unionist Labour Association (UULA) was elected just a week after he was wounded leading a mob in an attack on an isolated Catholic area in East Belfast. Not one of the Labour candidates was elected: the Unionists made a clean sweep and the twelve Irish Nationalists who were elected were mandated not to attend Parliament.

At the second election, which was held in April 1925, the Orange mobs and intimidation were not so much in evidence. Moreover, the worsening conditions of the unemployed and the increased number of the destitute provided the stimulus needed by the Independent Unionists, who usually supported labour politics, as well as the Labour Party, to have members elected to Parliament.

This trend was too dangerous to the Unionist strategy and before the next election in May 1929, steps to correct it had to be taken. Craig, as Prime Minister, moved an Amendment to the Government of Ireland Act which abolished the system of proportional representation in Ulster elections. In the course of his speech he compounded the strategy when he said:

> Proportional Representation submerges and clouds the issue. At election times, the people do not really understand what danger may result if they make a mistake when it comes to third, fourth, fifth or sixth preference... What I hold is, if the Ulster people are ever going – and I pray God they may not – into a Dublin Parliament, they should understand that they are voting to enter a Dublin Parliament, and not be led in by any trick of a complicated electoral system, such as Proportional Representation.[10]

The Unionists had no difficulty in carrying the proposed change through the legislative process even though there was considerable doubt about its constitutionality. The result was that the alternative parties to the two traditional ones virtually disappeared for the next sixteen years.

When the First World War ended and the soldiers came back to Belfast, Unionist domination of Ulster affairs no longer looked to be a foregone conclusion. Lloyd George's promises were not being kept and subsequent disappointment was proving a useful recruiting agent for the Labour Party. The Unionists had a genuine reason to fear that their majority would be swept away on a groundswell of support for

Labour's policies.

Things were brought to a head on 14 January 1919, when 20,000 workers from the heavy engineering shops in Belfast went on strike for a reduction in the working week to forty-four hours. The strike was part of a United Kingdom campaign to make room for ex-servicemen. Every major shop in Belfast, including gas, electricity and essential government services, came out in a massive demonstration of solidarity. A further 20,000 were laid off as a result. The strikers were ordered back by their cross-channel leaders when they realised that the whole strike movement was on the verge of defeat. In Belfast the story had been entirely different however. The employers were brought to their knees only to be saved by the fortuitous intervention of British union leaders' instructions to end the strike.[11]

On May Day 1919 at least 60,000 workers marched to the Ormeau Park in Belfast for a celebration meeting. In the Belfast Corporation election at the beginning of 1920 Labour recorded an unprecedented 20 per cent of the total vote, electing thirteen councillors in the process. There seemed little doubt that Labour and the working class of Belfast were on the march at last.[12]

The same political upheaval was happening in almost every city in Britain in 1919. Troops had marched to 10 Downing Street in protest against the conditions and delays of their demobilisation and there was unrest amongst the police. The Cabinet feared a revolt in Glasgow and sent English troops with tanks to cope with the situation.

A special report was prepared for the Cabinet by the Directorate of Intelligence (Home Office) entitled 'A Survey of Revolutionary feeling during the year 1919'. It stated 'they [referring to the mass of working men] have ocular proof of the fact that the employer class spend money lavishly and that the price of everything which the working man buys has risen enormously'. A list appended to the report showed the causes which the writer believed had contributed to the revolutionary feeling. It included 'foolish and dangerous ostentation of the rich', 'profiteering', 'a left-wing press' and 'the influence of extreme trade unionism'. Bonar Law, later Prime Minister of a Conservative Government, stated in the subsequent discussion in Cabinet that he thought the lack and poor quality of beer had had an unsettling effect on the steady men.[13]

In the immediate post-war local government elections Labour made considerable gains, winning control of most of the major cities throughout Britain.

The report to the Cabinet had struck the right note. Employers who had become rich on profits made in wartime production were suddenly unpopular. Belfast ex-servicemen were no different from their comrades in other cities: they were saying the same things about the employing class with equal bitterness.

The Unionists were greatly alarmed by the implications of their working classes 'spurning flags and seeking bread'. They were under no illusions as to the effect new political issues and realigned political forces would have on their ability to control the local state apparatus. They realised, moreover, that their fundamental strategy, which was based on keeping alight a militant anti-Catholicism, was at risk unless the whole course of current events could be reversed.

Sir Edward Carson, MP, the main Unionist leader, was already campaigning against the trend towards Labour by exaggerating the consequences for Britain of the Bolshevik take-over in Russia. Like his Conservative colleagues he was frightened that revolution, spreading throughout the whole of Europe in countries like Russia, Bavaria, Hungary and parts of Germany, would take root in Britain. In Glasgow there had been deep unrest amongst workers since 1915 which culminated in riots in January 1919. It was no comfort to Carson to know that a primary object of the rioters, apart from seeking a basic forty-four-hour week, was to maintain a class struggle until the wage system had been overthrown and industrial democracy obtained.[14]

Indeed, in the following month the Conservative Cabinet set up an Industrial Unrest Committee which had discussions with Sir Hugh Trenchard (Chief of Air Staff) on what steps the RAF could take to deal with the labour unrest. Trenchard's reticence was pushed aside by the Prime Minister, Lloyd George, who presumed they could use machine guns and drop bombs! Bonar Law felt that potential battalions of stockbrokers, who were to be found in every town, would be a loyal fighting class.[15]

Strike-breaking organisations were set up by Conservatives throughout the length and breadth of the United Kingdom to establish the means of transporting supplies in the event of a general strike. Propaganda machinery was created and used extensively by Government supporters in immediate counter activity.

Carson recognised that in Belfast he had something more substantial with which to contend. He helped to found the British Empire Union which would draw Unionist support on a wide basis in the hope that it could be used, if all else failed, as a bourgeois counter to the rapidly growing working-class radicalism. He knew that a bourgeois organisation like that would have very little effect on the newly found unity of the Belfast workers. He knew also that any attack on this unity had to come from inside the workers movement to have any success. He commenced by recruiting the skilled workers of the shipyard into the Ulster Unionist Labour Association which had been formed in April 1914. His intention was to use the UULA to purge the trade union movement of 'Bolsheviks' and Republicans. Within days of their formation members of the UULA were echoing Carson's sentiments and blaming unemployment on the tens of thousands of Catholics, who, they claimed, had pilfered jobs while 'ex-Service Protestants had been defending the Motherland'.[16]

Between 13–16 July 1920, the columns of Belfast Unionist newspapers were filled with anonymous letters complaining that Ulster Protestants had been asleep while Catholics had 'peacefully penetrated' workshops and left them homeless, jobless and helpless; processions and demonstrations were no good: 'Protestants must act now,' the letters proclaimed.

A meeting of all workers in the shipyard was arranged for lunchtime on 21 July. Men attended armed with guns and clubs and were told by the speakers to look for Catholics and drive them out of their place of work. The speakers at the meeting used as their text a speech made by Carson several days before at the celebration of Prince William of Orange's victory over King James at the Boyne River in 1690. Carson, attacking the labour leaders, referred to them as the 'Trojan Horse' of the IRA.

This speech was used by Unionist followers in the shipyard as justification to attack trade union leaders like James Baird, Sam Kyle and Charles McKay who were beaten and expelled along with Catholics from the shipyard. James Baird who was also a Belfast City Councillor wrote a letter to the Dublin *Evening Telegraph* (11 November 1920) describing the events of that day:

On 21 July and on succeeding dates, every Roman Catholic was expelled from the shipyard and other works. A number were flung into the river and, while struggling for life, were pelted with rivets and washers; others were brutally beaten but the majority, learning of the fate of their fellows, escaped, leaving behind costly tools and personal belongings. Almost 10,000 workers are at present affected and on several occasions men have attempted to resume work only to find 'loyal' men still determined to keep them out.

The trouble spread like wild-fire throughout Belfast, catching the Catholic population completely unawares. A special correspondent, writing in the *Daily News* on 31 August 1920, reported that all businesses owned by Belfast Catholics, except those located in the Catholic stronghold of the Falls, were destroyed.

The total number of serious conflagrations during the last six days now stands at 180 or considerably more than one per hour over the whole period: if small firms were added, the total would be easily doubled. The value of damage for Belfast would add to over £1 million.

Meanwhile Catholic families were being evicted in their hundreds from homes in the Protestant quarters of Belfast. Several thousand families were driven by Orange mobs to seek shelter in already congested Nationalist areas; hundreds had to lodge in schoolhouses, stores and stalls. Some slept in tents on land adjacent to churches. Large numbers of unlucky ones had to wander the street by day in fruitless search for shelter and to sleep in the open by night. A few Protestants from Catholic areas made friendly exchanges with Catholics for houses in Protestant quarters.[17]

Madam Charlotte Despard, sister of Sir John French, the last Viceroy of Ireland before the Free State was established in 1920, described, in a letter, a visit to the Catholic enclave of Ballymacarret in Belfast shortly after the new regime had come to power.

At that time Belfast was a really frightening place, where Catholics were regular victims of pogroms from police and paramilitaries, who operated with the tacit permission of the Stormont Government... Having visited many panic-stricken families, inspected their houses riddled with bullet holes, I stood talking with some of the women. Everything was quiet. The people stood about in little groups before their doors. The children were playing. Suddenly there was a pistol shot fired from an armoured car. Panic followed and the children ran into any open door. I was drawn by trembling women into the cottage of an ex-soldier, a man who had fought in Belgium and Gallipoli. Volley after volley from rifles and machine guns swept the street and this went on with brief intervals for an hour and a half.

Charlotte stormed into the office of the Minister of Home Affairs, Sir Dawson Bates. But he just commented that the B Specials were 'a fine body of men' and rudely turned his back on her. Nothing daunted she sought an interview with the Prime Minister, Sir James Craig, and addressed him in what can only be described as prophetic words. 'Go on as you are doing', she told him, 'give your legalised gunmen carte blanche to shoot, maim and insult their fellow townsmen and to destroy their homes; keep thousands of men idle and as sure as day succeeds night retribution in an awful form will come to you.'[18]

Madam Despard was echoed to some extent later in the Northern Ireland Parliament by Lord Londonderry.

> A section of those who saw eye to eye with the Government [and] were implicated in outrages as reprehensible as those committed by Sinn Fein were placing the Government in an impossible situation. When negotiating with British Ministers he should like to appear before them with clean hands. That was by no means the case now.

Thousands of workers lost their jobs in the engineering factories of Harland & Wolff Ltd, Musgrave & Co. Ltd, Workman Clarks (Shipbuilders); James Mackie & Sons, Davidson & Co. (Sirocco Works), Coombe, Barbour & Lawson (Textile Engineers); and McLaughlin & Harvey (Civil Engineers & Builders).

On 22 July 1920 the troubles were debated in Westminster and Carson congratulated the shipyard workers on their action. He had already praised them at a public meeting in the shipyard on getting rid of 'Papists and rotten Prods' from the workshops. ('Rotten Prods' was Craig's description of the trade union leaders.) The debate at Westminster was noteworthy because of the assertion made by J.M. Clyne, MP, that Ulster operatives and workers divided were more easily exploited than when united. Speaking earlier in the same debate James Sexton, MP, general secretary of the National Union of Dock Labourers, said:

> Men who have worked together harmoniously for years and years, Protestant and Catholic, on the docks of Belfast are today divided into two hostile sections. The Protestant element, influenced by the 12th July outrage are today driving the Catholic

element of the same Union from the work at the docks.

Sexton and Clyne were obviously referring to Carson's speech on 12 July at the Orange Demonstration in Belfast in which he said;

These men who come forward posing as the friends of Labour care no more about Labour than does the man in the moon. Their real object, and the real insidious nature of their propaganda, is that they may mislead and bring about disunity amongst our own people, and in the end before we know where we are, we may find ourselves in the same bondage and slavery as is the rest of Ireland in the South and West. We must proclaim today clearly that, come what will and be the consequences what they may, we in Ulster will tolerate no Sinn Fein – no Sinn Fein organisation, no Sinn Fein methods.[19]

Carson was identifying Sinn Fein, Catholicism and Labour as being the same intolerable thing as far as the Orange Order and the Unionist Party were concerned.

The employers' attitude to the innocent victims was summed up by Mr Davidson, chairman of the Board of Directors of Sirocco Works, at a lunch-hour meeting with the labour force when he stated that he looked upon the expelled workers as Sinn Feiners, as nothing short of German Huns and Russian Bolsheviks in disguise and whose traitorous enmity to King and Country was only equalled by their murderous disposition towards all who were loyal Unionists.[20]

Rev. Dr McRory, Catholic Bishop of Down and Connor, had a better understanding of the situation when he forwarded a contribution of £100 to the Committee for Expelled Workers. He wrote that 'it was a hard fact that their fellow workers had expelled them even though it was by political and capitalistic influence on them. It was unholy Carsonite incitement of the 12 July that caused it... the politicians were bullies and sleek abettors who talk glibly of civil and religious liberty!'

An emergency resolution which had been submitted by the Standing Orders Committee of the TUC at its conference in September 1920 was carried. It said that 'in their anxiety to uphold the Union Jack in Belfast men were prevented from working for their religious and political opinions' and it instructed the Parliamentary Committee to call together immediately the executives of the various trade unions affected by the recent disturbances in Belfast with a view to their taking a common line of action for the reinstatement of all trade unionists expelled from their work in the Belfast area.

The emergency resolution emphasised what was the corner stone of trade union objectives, i.e., 'the necessity of securing justice and equality for all members of the Trade Union movement regardless of class, colour or creed'. It was an unshakeable principle, common to all craft union constitutions, that all workers expelled from Belfast factories would be restored to their jobs by Union effort.

Apart from the Amalgamated Society of Carpenters and Joiners who expelled 2,000 members for refusing to support the return to work of their Catholic fellow members, unions chose to ignore the expulsions. Repercussions from this action were ever afterwards to have serious effects on the trade union movement and on society as a whole in Belfast. By ignoring the principle of equality in their industrial relationships trade unions in Belfast deprived themselves of the opportunities to develop the philosophy which proved so essential to the trade union movement in Britain in creating an effective political form. Sensitivity to the main issues of equality would have driven the unions away from the Unionist Government which practised blatant inequalities on such a large scale.

A delegation of three from the Parliamentary sub-committee was appointed to find a settlement. They met a wide range of people, from the expelled workers to the managements of the engineering firms. But they were completely lost after the managements insisted that they were in business to make ships and were not concerned with the religious or political views of work people.[21]

The executives of eighteen unions met in London on 26 January 1921 to consider the Belfast troubles. No progress resulted until the engineering employers imposed a wage cut of twelve shillings per week and the workers united to withdraw their labour in resistance to the wage reductions.[22]

The compromise arrived at in the face of the wage cut came to nothing. Expelled workers never returned to their jobs because those still at work never pressed for their reinstatement and also because there were fewer jobs available.

More importantly it was by now clear that the policy of the new Government was to provide jobs for its own Protestant people.

The Belfast bourgeoisie were always alert to the need to protect their interests. And they were no less alert to the pressure building up

51

in the shipbuilding industry throughout the United Kingdom for the introduction of a basic forty-hour week at the same rate of wages to absorb the thousands of ex-servicemen who could not find jobs. The Scottish TUC and a number of trades councils in shipbuilding areas had resolutions on the TUC agenda that looked certain, with the widespread support promised, to be part of Labour Party programme for the next election.

In the midst of all the trouble, the Belfast employers decided to pre-empt minor union demands by cutting back on the earnings levels of their workers in the shipbuilding and engineering factories.

High wages in the engineering industries had been causing employers acute concern since November 1919, when the Interim Court of Arbitration had awarded the Federation of Engineering Trades, representing shipyard workers, five shillings per week against Harland & Wolff and Workman Clark. The award applied to other engineering firms as well. This brought the Belfast weekly wage rates to 87s. 10d. According to a Parliamentary Report in 1921 the rates of wages in Belfast for engineering work were 1s. 6d. higher than any other workplace in Ireland, Scotland and in some other regions in England.

Fearing the effects of high wages on their manufacturing costs, a high-powered delegation of Unionist industrialists met the Conservative Government in secret to urge them to pass labour affairs over to the new Northern Ireland administration. It was intended originally to retain finance, defence and labour matters at Westminster. The delegation had no difficulty in persuading the Conservatives to make the transfer, as, by that time, the Unemployment Insurance Fund was already in the red to the order of £5 million. However, the reason for the proposal to transfer labour matters to the Northern Ireland Government was to enable local industrialists to cut wages more substantially than was envisaged across the water where the workers were better organised to resist such cuts. In Northern Ireland they were too distracted by other and, according to the local bourgeoisie, 'more important matters of state', to resist wage cuts. In other words, while the Protestant worker was in uniform in the streets as an auxiliary policeman combating IRA activities, his employer was reducing his wages for the same patriotic motives.

Information about this visit to the Conservative Government was never made public until it slipped out inadvertently during the debate on the Unemployment Insurance Fund in the Northern Ireland

Parliament on 16 October 1924. Thompson Donald, a Labour Unionist, stated angrily that neither he nor Lord Carson, who were both MPs at Westminster at the time, agreed with the transfer of labour matters to Northern Ireland. They were of the opinion that it would lead to the unemployed in Northern Ireland receiving less unemployment insurance than the unemployed received in Britain under the same legislation.[23]

Donald by this time had realised that while he and his fellow workers were expelling the labour leadership from the engineering shops of Belfast, the bourgeoisie were engaged in covert activities to cut wages. They recognised that to do that the bourgeoisie had to get control of the Unemployment Insurance Fund and pay benefits out to the unemployed at a lower rate than was paid in Britain: wage rates could be reduced to a fraction above unemployment benefit levels. With the labour leadership gone from Belfast works, little resistance was mounted by the workers to the wage cuts.

The employers, having rid themselves of possible labour resistance commenced in earnest to reduce wages in a series of cuts which lasted throughout the early Twenties. By 1925, shipyard workers who had earlier earned 87s. for a forty-seven-hour week were left with wages of 47s. for the same hours. Of course the employers had ample assistance from government departments as well as from the Unionist Council in forcing wages downwards. It was felt by the bourgeoisie that this had to be done to counter the effects of the boycott of Northern goods and products by the Free State Government. That reply was fallacious as it disregarded the fact that the Free State was not a competitor nor a consumer of the North's shipyard and heavy engineering products; but Unionist workers as usual were taken in by it!

In any case, employers experienced no harassment from unions in reducing wages. According to reports in the press, there was little employee resistance in many areas. There was no legislation to protect wages and no desire on the Government's part to introduce any. It was a businessman's government that had successfully sold the idea to its supporters that the state could only exist if it could sell enough to enable it to pay its own way. Otherwise political enemies in Westminster, particularly within the growing Labour Party, might prefer to hive them off to the Free State. In addition to that, the diminution of production costs which had risen steeply during the war was warmly welcomed by the manufacturers and the Government. They believed that the reduction of labour costs would enable them to compete better and jobs would still be available for the skilled workers.

An example of the connivance to cut wages is contained in a circular letter which was sent out by the Ministry of Labour on 31 March 1924 to all employers in the Trade Board Register in Northern Ireland. The circular referred to an amendment to the Trade Board Act (Northern Ireland), introduced in 1923, which 'make a number of alterations to the administration of Trade Boards, designed to simplify and speed up wage-fixing machinery'. The Act was interpreted by the Ministries, according to the circular, in a way that would enable employers attached to the Trade Boards to take advantage of minimum rates of wages recently fixed by the Boards for learners and apprentices. Employers were informed that to be eligible for the sub-minimum rate, learners must hold certificates from the Trade Board. In the absence of these, *all workers* would come henceforth within the scope of determination of the Board of Trade in regard to rates of wages payable to adult workers and to other grades of learners and apprentices.

The implied aim of the circular was to precipitate a wages cutback, and it succeeded. Professor Henry of Queen's University, who was chairman of the Board and highly esteemed by the workers' leaders, resigned in protest at the issuing of this devious circular.[24] The leaders of the craft unions, patently informed before the circular was issued, welcomed it: the effects of the move were not manifest for months afterwards. By then it was too late to arrest the momentum of the wage-slide that had started in the wake of the first riots of 1920 and was carried on with the help of the Government.

The financial arrangements set out in the Government of Ireland Act, 1920, were that both Parliaments set up by the Act would secure sufficient financial resources of their own to pay for their own services and that an agreed sum would go towards the maintenance of Imperial Services. But it was not to work out like that in practice.

The Free State received virtual financial autonomy right from the beginning. Northern Ireland's financial powers and resources were entirely inadequate. The Northern Ireland Controller and Auditor General, in his first report on the Appropriation Account, stated that Britain controlled 88 per cent of the Northern Ireland revenue and 60 per cent of her expenditure. Again, in 1924, the Northern Ireland Select Committee of Public Accounts reported that the position was not satisfactory. It claimed to have no control of large sections of the revenue and expenditure and to have received no accounts from either.[25]

The calculations for Northern Ireland's expenditure on social services were worked out annually at the sum of £4. 2s. 0d. per head compared with that of £14. 13. 9d. per head in Britain. The calculation was unfair and Northern Ireland was placed at a clear disadvantage.[26]

These transactions between the Northern Ireland Finance Minister and the British Exchequer, for political reasons, have always been clouded in mystery. The Joint Exchequer Board which met once a year never published reports. It was taken for granted that the public had no right to know and seldom enquired into the details of the arrangements. It was only in general terms that Northern Ireland's revenue and expenditure were fixed and no further information was offered to the public for fear it would be used as propaganda against the Unionist Government.

The nearest that financial matters ever got to public attention was on that occasion when Lord Colwyn's Committee reported in 1925. This Committee, appointed by the British Government to recommend the scale of contribution annually to be made by Northern Ireland for Imperial services, fixed the principle that Northern Ireland, as long as it maintained taxation parity with Britain, was entitled to the same standard of social services. Under the provisions of the original Act all matters, apart from those pertaining to external defence and fiscal affairs, were transferred to the Northern Ireland Government.

Unemployment insurance, first set up in 1910, covered in its scope the entire United Kingdom. By 1920, after the economy had enjoyed a wartime boom period, the Unemployment Insurance Fund ran into deficit. By the time labour affairs were hived off to Northern Ireland, the fund was in the red to the tune of £160,000. In addition 25 per cent of the insured population was unemployed.

Without reserves, the Unemployment Insurance Fund in Northern Ireland soon ran into stormy weather. The Government was forced to devise a form of unconvenanted aid for the unemployed which they hoped would be recoverable when times improved and increased employment brought the Fund back to solvency. This uncovenanted fund gave the Government another opportunity to assist their supporters when they had exhausted their entitlement to benefit in the existing covenanted schemes. Payments from the Unemployment Insurance Fund to the unemployed were varied in application. The object was to apply the scheme in Northern Ireland to skilled workers while withholding benefit from all unemployed outside the engineering and allied trades. That meant drafting amendments to parity legislation to create devices that would get cash benefits to Unionist supporters when they were unemployed while depriving Catholics and labour supporters of benefits from the same sources.

The main device used was to divide the applications for benefit between those who were 'normally in insurable employment' and those who were 'not normally in insurable employment'. Insurable employment in this context referred to the shipbuilding and engineering industries. Other applications were subject to the discretion of the insurance officers in the Ministry of Labour. The unemployed who were qualified to receive payment were out of work for prolonged periods and it was necessary for the Minister of Commerce to devise a scheme, almost like the unemployment insurance scheme in Britain, to continue payments to their own supporters. This was named the Unemployment Insurance Bill and was given a second reading on 8 April 1924. This Bill was to enable the Ministry of Labour to give covenanted benefit to the unemployed covering a twenty-six week period, followed by a twenty-six week period of uncovenanted benefit, which could be extended further at the Minister's discretion. To consolidate this, the Government issued an official memorandum on what it was doing for labour.

> While the payment of benefit to persons who, through no fault of their own, cannot obtain work, is obviously necessary, it is by common consent not so good as the provision of work and accordingly the Government, with the cordial assistance of local authorities throughout Ulster, has initiated relief works, the capital cost of which is over £2,615,375. Government funds are subsidising these works to the extent of over £664,356. Employment has been found by this means for some thousands of men and at the present moment there are about 2,659 men directly employed on them, while an unknown, but certainly large number, is employed indirectly. In addition, the Loans Guarantee Acts provide special facilities for employers for expenditure on capital reconstruction and the like, and, as a result of the operation of these Acts, seven big ships have been built in Belfast and more are likely to follow.

In Britain twenty-eight Unemployment Acts were introduced between 1920 and 1934. Nothing like that was attempted in Northern

Ireland. When the Blanesburgh Committee reported to Parliament in 1927 and recommended that extended benefit and standard benefit be integrated, it was still kept separate in Northern Ireland. In 1929, when it was decided to abolish the Poor Law in England, pay cash benefits as a right and make them a direct charge on taxation, Northern Ireland chose to ignore the legislative changes even though the principle of parity on this legislation had been established in 1925.

Of course, there were political reasons for ignoring the legislation. The Unionist Government understood quite well that once the payment of relief was made to the destitute and unemployed as of right, the Catholic opposition, with larger families, would increase its votes and in the fullness of time replace them as the administrators of Northern Ireland. This development had to be avoided. Their difficulty, as always, arose from doing it without upsetting their own working-class supporters.

Unemployment figures for Northern Ireland were usually twice as high as in Britain:

Unemployed as percentage of total population

	Northern Ireland	Great Britain
1922	22.9	14.1
1926	23.3	12.3
1930	24.3	15.8
1934	23.9	16.6
1938	28.0	12.8

(Source: Department of Labour, Northern Ireland)

Doubts had always been cast on the Northern Ireland figures by Opposition speakers during Parliamentary debates. The Opposition MPs always insisted that they were higher and that the records kept referred only to those in receipt of unemployment benefit and that thoe who received no benefits (estimated at 10,000 to 12,000 extra) were excluded. These extra figures encompassed the long-term unemployed of the working-class areas of West, North and East Belfast and landless labourers in areas of Fermanagh, Tyrone and Armagh.

Unionist strategy was to force these unwanted citizens to emigrate. To avoid Westminster's attention this had to be done in an undramatic way. Special powers and police excesses were often counter-productive for this purpose. Economic pressure by stealth, like the deprivation of relief to people in distress, was a perfect instrument to move 'undesirables' onwards.

Reliable figures on emigration from Northern Ireland were hard to come by during the early years of Unionist rule. None of the sources which were to be available for this purpose later existed to provide information on emigration at this time. Few authorities in this field, apart from Professor Brendan Walsh of the Irish Social and Economic Institute, have tried to put a figure on Northern Ireland emigration. Brendan Walsh put the loss of population from Ulster due to emigration from 1926 to 1937 at 12 per cent: Catholics, 9 per cent and Protestants, 3 per cent.

Northern Ireland population in 1926	1,256,561
Natural increase (excess of births over deaths)	80,835
1926 population plus natural increase	1,337,396
Enumerated 1937 population	1,279,745
Net movement outwards	57,651
Annual net movement outwards	5,241
Annual net movement of Catholics outwards	3,930
Annual net movement of Protestants outwards	1,310

This information, published in the *Ulster Year Book*, 1950, was provided by masters of vessels entering or leaving British ports. It is based on the last place of residence of each passenger. It does not take into account the number of emigrants to the Irish Republic or to major British cities but it is useful in that it indicates in religious terms the number of those who were recorded as having emigrated from Northern Ireland. It ignores the fact however that the names of those who did emigrate were often retained on census lists by relatives and neighbours for electoral purposes.

The figures are not completely accurate as the birth rate for Catholics was regularly reported as twice as high as that of Protestants. Larger numbers of Catholics ought to have been included in the totals. The Northern Ireland Government, for obvious reasons, had no monitoring process for families moving to the South of Ireland or to England to escape from the extreme violence of the Orange mobs or the later institutional violence of the state. The Government had a vested interest in not recording information of this nature because of the possibility of a sharp response from Westminster or from the Irish Government in Dublin.

What is known, however, is that, from its earliest days, the Ministry of Labour concentrated heavily on forcing Catholic males of all ages to leave seeking jobs elsewhere. A senior government official, writing in 1978 of his lifetime of service in the Northern Ireland Civil Service, said that when he started in the service in the late Twenties he and his colleagues struggled to devise schemes for sending men and youths abroad to where work was available. How successful these schemes were can be judged by a letter which was published in *The Labour Opposition* in January 1926. An emigrant in Moosejaw in Canada wrote to warn prospective emigrants from Northern Ireland that those coming to Canada by assisted passage would have difficulty in finding work except on farms at poor pay. The writer said that it seemed to him that the Northern Ireland Government wanted a lot of people away out of sight quickly.[26]

The Government realised the importance to its strategy of making it easy for families to emigrate. They paid for families from West Belfast to go to Birmingham, Coventry and London. Single Catholic men were sent to Australia and single Protestant men to Canada and New Zealand. Unemployed shipyard workers were offered temporary employment each summer in border areas like Fermanagh, thus enabling them to receive full unemployment benefit when they returned, after the harvest, to Belfast.

The setting-up of the state of Northern Ireland proved to be a big help to the bourgeoisie in carrying out their strategy which coincided almost exactly with the wishes of the Government. By acquiring control of state power, they were able to legalise the use and amend the machinery of government at all levels to make the strategy work. They had two fronts on which to operate. The first one was to turn Protestant anger on to Catholics, claiming they were at war with the state. Protestant support was necessary to help to defeat 'the enemy within its gates'. This part of the strategy, as in the past, was successful. Catholics were deprived of jobs, homes and relief from distress, while the main trade union and labour movement looked on without concern.

The second used the same logic, for different reasons, on the Protestant skilled and able-bodied unemployed, to persuade them to accept less than the standard of economic and social security that workers received across the water. The skilled workers, and, to some extent, the Protestant population as a whole seemed satisfied to receive preferment over Catholics, at the cost of parity with the unemployed in Britain. They acquiesced in, as well as supported, the Government's blatant discrimination against their fellow citizens. It was thus that the strategy as well as the structures of social control for securing the interests of the bourgeoisie in Northern Ireland were established.

Part II

5
The Poor Law in Ireland

The Poor Law was introduced in England to prevent the spread of agitation in rural areas. The reasons for its introduction into Ireland four years later in 1838 were different. Some knowledge of these reasons and indeed of the background and growth of the Poor Law are essential to understand the hypothesis of this study.

Prior to the Act of Union in 1801 measures enacted by the local Parliament to deal with poverty aimed not so much at the relief of poverty as at the punishment and control of the poor. Indeed in the seventeenth and eighteenth centuries, penalties for vagrancy and begging included commitment to a 'House of Correction' with 'moderate whipping' to press the point home, transportation to the Colonies and even death to the incorrigibles.

After the Act of Union in 1801 a number of Acts of a more humane nature were passed by Parliament at Westminster concerning the relief of the poor in Ireland. These served only as temporary measures until the more significant Act of 1838 was introduced as a consequence of the comprehensive attempt in England to deal with the problems of destitution. Thus Irish Poor Law, right from its beginning, was similar in principle and in object, though not in its application, because of the extreme variations in the living conditions of the people.[1]

The Act of 1805 had great practical effect on the conditions of the poor in that it led to the setting-up of dispensaries to provide medicine and medical aid and to the building of infirmaries and hospitals with money raised by County Grand Juries. It also gave Grand Juries the right to levy subscriptions from the population of each county within certain limits, to meet the costs of building and administering the services. This Act was subsequently amended to enable Grand Juries to build lunatic asylums and fever hospitals as well as to make and pay for the appointments of Health Inspectors for each county.

In 1819 a Select Committee of the House of Commons was set up to enquire into the condition of the labouring poor in Ireland.[2] The Committee reported several times over the next few years. Members of the Committee visited Ireland frequently during this period and were able to study at first hand the acute distress caused by the severe depression in 1822.

This hardship arose from economic circumstances occasioned when Ireland changed her role from that of corn importer to that of grain and livestock exporter. These economic circumstances imposed a new emphasis on tillage; pasture farming was reduced to that of dry cattle. In its wake came the establishment of the potato as the staple food of the people. As well as being a cheap and nutritious food for people and livestock, the potato had other valuable qualities. It cleaned and restored the soil and it enabled the landowners to multiply the number of small-holdings on their land thereby creating for themselves a large labour force to whom they did not have to pay wages.[3]

The Select Committee's reports covered a number of periods in the early nineteenth century in which widespread distress was caused by the failure of the potato crop. The reports succeeded in highlighting the fact that there was no deficiency in other crops nor any real scarcity of food; prices for corn and oatmeal were moderate, but people simply had not the means to buy them. Records were produced to show that at times of scarcity the exports of grain from Irish ports within the distressed area were considerable.

Evidence attached to the reports indicated that the people were living in wretched conditions and in a state of the utmost misery. Many of the families whose homes had been visited by the Committee had no bedclothes; a quantity of straw thrown on the floor served as a bed on which they all lay in their working clothes. Their cabins were made of mud and contained no furniture. The main work of those people living close to the sea consisted of carrying sand and seaweed inland for miles to fertilise the land while those living inland were forced at certain seasons of the year to quit their homes to get employment abroad.

Irish landlords, according to witnesses who appeared before the inquiry of the Select Committee, employed labour on the basis that they got unlimited work from them in return for a one-room cabin, a potato patch, a portion of a bog for peat, any dung to be found on the farmer's land and 'a run of a pig'.

Labour was paid at the rate of 6d to 8d per day: when 'diet' was received by the workers only 4d to 6d was paid. Accounts were kept of days worked, usually by tallysticks. Wage disputes were frequent and many had to be concluded under direction from the local Quarter Sessions. Rev. Somers Payne of Cork County, giving evidence to a Poor Law Inquiry in 1836, said that he had been a Peace Commissioner for nearly 30 years and had never sat in a court without hearing of some act of aggression on the part of the farmer towards his labourer.

Complaints books in rural areas during the years 1825–40 were mainly filled with disputes in which labourers were reported as 'hauling farmers before the Petty Sessions to answer charges of withholding wages'.[4]

Bound labourers generally received half an acre of potato ground in return for their labour. But another and more restrictive system of hire existed for casual labourers which was known as 'taking land in conacre'. Rent was taken by the farmer out of all subsequent crops while the labourer who worked the land was allowed only a portion of the immediate potato crop which he cultivated.

By 1832, information gathered by Parliament on the extreme poverty that existed in England and Ireland, as well as on the predictable consequences of a failure to provide relief in the aftermath of the labourers' revolt of 1830, led to the appointment of a Parliamentary Commission which was required to report regularly to the House of Commons. It was intended that the Commission's work would extend to Ireland and Commissioners were appointed with that purpose in view.

The Irish Commissioners duly reported back in 1836, recommending the creation of a Board to plan and supervise wide schemes of national improvements which would be financed by state loans and local rates. A Commission of Poor Law for Ireland would be set up which would supervise the Board and be responsible for the care of infirmed, aged and lunatic poor.

The evidence attached to the report stated that, unlike workers in Britain, those in Ireland were forced to look to the agricultural sector for support. Agricultural families in Britain in 1831 represented only one-quarter of the population; in Ireland they represented two-thirds. Moreover, there were five agricultural labourers in Ireland for every one in Britain.

The Commissioners in their earlier reports said that it was impossible for the able-bodied to provide for food, in the face of sickness, loss of employment, old age and destitution. They assessed that, for thirty weeks each year, no less than 575,000 would be out of work and the distressed would add a further 1,800,000, bringing the total to almost 2,400,000. They reckoned that the cost of relieving that number in workhouses would be around 4,000,000 shillings, which was equal to the country's national revenue.[5]

Lord George Russell, the Minister responsible for introducing the legislation, was convinced that the cost of relieving nearly 2½ million destitutes would be too great an obstacle for him to get the Bill through Westminster. Accordingly, Sir George Nicholls, one of the English Commissioners, was recruited to go to Ireland to examine the Irish Commissioners' evidence and submit a set of recommendations which Russell could guide through Parliament.

Nicholls, taking his cue from what he believed the Minister would be able to push through Parliament, reported back in favour of a severely limited system of Poor Relief to which the destitute were to have no legal right. A number of workhouses were to be built and maintained by local rate. There would be no Outdoor Relief, only that provided within the walls of the workhouse. Nicholls' own personal view was evident in the report when he declared at the conclusion that 'the squalor and poverty of the Irish to a large extent were of their own making'.[6]

As a result of Nicholls' suggestions, Lord Russell was able to introduce a Bill on 13 February 1837, but the Bill was aborted because of the death of William IV. This lapse allowed Nicholls to visit Ireland again to see whether the English Poor Law system could be established there. He reported back within a month to the effect that he could see no insurmountable difficulties.

In the course of this second report Nicholls referred to the operation of a poor law system which he found already operating on a voluntary basis in several areas of Ulster. He mentioned in particular that the townlands of Monaghan, Newry, Coleraine and the cities of Armagh, Derry and Belfast had already made provision for relieving the destitute, thus recognising the principle of the English Poor Law that the community had a duty to protect its members against perishing from want. He described the difference between the north and the south and west of Ireland by stating that the destitute in the south and west depended for support upon the class immediately above them, i.e. the small cottiers and cultivators, but in Ulster sympathy existed between all the classes of society and led to the cost provision for the needy being better distributed over the whole of the community.

The Irish Poor Law Act was passed as expected in 1838 and its implementation was placed in the hands of Nicholls who was required to reside in Ireland to supervise its workings at close range. The Act required that Ireland be divided into 130 Unions in which workhouses would be built to cater for the destitute of each area. A Board of Guardians, elected by the ratepayers, complemented by the County JPs, would run them. The power to levy a Poor Rate on the local landlords and their tenants and to appoint and pay officials, was transferred to the Boards.

Nicholls, with two others, was appointed a Commissioner and stayed in Ireland for four years to establish the system. He insisted on the rigid application of the principle that relief in the workhouse should be given at a rate less than the support which could be obtained by independent means.

On entry, paupers were segregated by age and sex. Husbands and wives were separated. The Commissioners made certain by their regulations that conditions should not be such as to invite the aged and the infirm to seek refuge within the workhouse. Diet consisted of oatmeal, buttermilk and potatoes. Soup was given out twice weekly and no tobacco or alcohol was allowed in any form.

Under Section 41 of this Act, preference had to be given to the aged, the sick, and destitute children, before other destitute persons from within the Union could be considered for entry.

The English Act enabled the Commissioners to make provision for Outdoor Relief in the event of economic depression and to deal with special problems in special cases. Under the Irish Act there was no such possibility. Relief was effectively confined to the aged, the sick, and destitute children from the Union area who were admitted to the workhouse. Once the workhouse was full, the obligation to help other destitute persons was removed.

By January 1844, 43,293 persons were receiving Indoor Relief; of these 52 per cent were children under the age of sixteen; 27 per cent were disabled due to chronic sickness, age or other infirmity, and of the remaining 21 per cent, seven out of every ten were women.[7]

The system had more than its share of growing pains outside Ulster. There were many difficulties created in the collection of the Poor Rate. Ratepayers, especially during the times of depression, could not pay. Police, and occasionally the military, were called out in support of collectors. In Tuam and Castlereagh the Boards which had refused point-blank to collect their rates and open workhouses were dissolved after legal proceedings were instituted by the Poor Law Commissioners.

The theory of the Poor Law system was to place the burden of relieving the poor on the landlords who would pay rates to cover the costs of that relief. It worked well enough in England but not so well in Ireland, for the obvious reason that Ireland had not a cash economy.

In spite of all this, a relief system was built up stretching from one end of the country to the other which, according to the Commission's report, could cope adequately with the number of destitute needing Indoor Relief at any given time. The number was set arbitrarily at 100,000 paupers and ignored entirely the possibility of a famine on an immense scale if the potato crop failed. This, of course, had threatened on a number of occasions during the previous twenty years. By 1846 the worst of these predictions came to pass and Ireland was hit catastrophically by a series of failures of the potato crop that left millions of people without food.

There was no way that the Poor Law system could deal with the massive problems created by recurring famines, and the ensuing famine fever, over a period of several years. Hundreds of thousands died of starvation and fever. People emigrated in their thousands throughout these terrible years. Two and a half million people died or were forced to emigrate during the period of the Great Famine.[8] The famine was of unprecedented severity over a sustained period, during which the Government was forced to give grants on an ex-gratia basis to local authorities for the purpose of financing public employment schemes. These resources were supplemented by the opening of soup kitchens in areas to the south and west of Ireland where the number of families starving was greatest.

Meanwhile, the Commissioners were under relentless pressure from all sides to expand the scope of their activities. As a result, they pleaded desperately with the Government behind the scenes for authority to widen their powers to deal more flexibly with relief schemes for the able-bodied.

As requested by the Commissioners, the Poor Law Act which followed extended the powers and responsibilities of the Commission. This was the first occasion that Outdoor Relief was paid for under Poor Law Administration in Ireland. It enabled a Special Relief Committee to be set up which would draw up lists of destitute people in various areas and estimate the costs of providing them with the necessities of life. These lists were to be monitored by a Finance Committee on behalf of the Lord Lieutenant who would approve payments to them through the agency of the Boards of Guardians.

A further Act, closely related to the first one, entitled the Poor Relief Extension Act 1847, was introduced. This Act empowered Boards to grant Outdoor or Indoor Relief to the aged, the infirm, the sick, the poor and to widows with two dependent children. It also empowered the Boards to give out food to able-bodied poor for a limited period. The following table taken from the Poor Law Report issued 29 September 1854 indicates the importance of both Acts in mitigating the fatal effects of the last months of the famine.

	Annual expenditure £	Ann. population relieved indoor	Ann. population relieved outdoor	Total population relieved
1847	803,684	417,139	–	–
1848	1,732,597	610,463	1,433,042	2,043,505
1849	2,177,651	932,284	1,210,482	2,142,766
1850	1,430,108	805,702	368,565	1,174,267
1851	1,141,647	707,443	47,914	755,357
1852	883,267	504,864	14,911	519,775
1853	785,718	396,436	13,232	409,668

The ratio of destitutes was much higher in Ireland than in England. Industrialisation in Britain had created a more voluminous cash flow which enabled the large labour force there to take more care of impoverished relations. In Ireland, however, there was little industrialisation outside Belfast. Hence, there was little money in circulation to help the destitute outside the workhouse.

By 1850, however, a sharp fall in the numbers of destitute requiring Outdoor Relief was recorded. Crops once more were healthy and plentiful. The overall situation gave the impression of returning to normal. Certainly the pressure on the workhouses began to subside. House rules were applied to inmates in a less severe fashion, the staff behaving more benignly to those in need of care and relief. Food was of better quality; milk and bread were added to the diet. For those inmates who could afford it a little tobacco and snuff were permitted. Finally, elderly couples could share small compartments that were constructed specially for that purpose.[9]

The economy continued to show an improvement according to the reports drafted by the Poor Law Commissioners for the years after 1855. They recorded that deaths in the workhouses of Ulster had fallen from five in 1855 to two per year from 1856 onwards. These reports indicated economic improvements throughout Ireland. Wages rose in the agricultural sector and more employment became available. Paupers had virtually disappeared from Ulster apart from Belfast. It was odd indeed that a highly industrialised city like Belfast with its capacity to assimilate large numbers of workers annually could still have so many destitute while other areas, including its own hinterland, had so few. The clear implication of this lack of capacity to help the distress was that they wanted to deter the destitute from rural areas in the south and west of Ireland from coming to Belfast. In Belfast patrols, paid for out of the rates, swept the main streets of vagrants, bringing them before the town's two Resident Magistrates. No mercy was shown to the vagrants. They were sent by the RM to the House of Correction, usually once a week, where they had their heads shaven before incarceration. Belfast was particularly vigilant and rigorous in its treatment of vagrants who, fearing their fate at the hands of the patrols, tended to leave the town at the earliest opportunity.

The ninth Poor Relief Report, issued in 1881, contained a section which stated that Belfast had an undiseased potato crop, the best for thirty years, that wages were averaging 13s. 0d. per week and that the only distress anticipated was a possible demand for relief from local mill workers. It also referred to the fact that the Belfast Union could not meet the increased demand for workhouse accommodation, due no doubt in these years to the large numbers moving into the city from the hinterland west of the River Bann where population decreases tended to correspond with population increases in Belfast.

According to this Poor Law Report, Ulster consisted of forty-four Unions which were divided into 214 dispensary areas; the population was in excess of 1,800,000; Poor Law evaluation amounted to £178,970; and the number of people receiving relief was 106,765, the average cost per head being 2s. 11¾d.

The lot of the Irish tenants improved considerably with the passing of the Land Act of 1881. They had less rent to pay and their increasing ability to consume home-grown products with remittances sent by emigrants, brought to them a feeling of security hitherto unknown by their social class.

Events soon to effect the functioning of the Poor Law in Ireland were, by this time, in full flood in Britain. Reports on destitution were being brought to Parliament from a number of sources. The extension of the franchise, the formation of trade unions for the labouring classes, allied with attempts to measure poverty by reformers like Charles Booth, the Webbs and Octavia Hill, brought a Liberal Government to Westminster on a programme of radical reforms that were designed to meet the needs of recurring cycles of distress throughout the British Isles.[10]

The election promises of the Liberals, some of them made to woo the support of the Irish Parliamentary Party, led to a new and more significant piece of legislation called the Local Government (Ireland) Act 1898. Under this Act, county councils, rural and borough councils and urban district councils were formed and given the responsibility of levying, collecting and spending rates. It was set out in the Act that one half of any expenditure incurred in pursuance of an Order under Section 3 of the Act could be levied off the county at large. The total amount of any such expenditure should not exceed three pence in the pound on the rateable value of the county. The Guardians could obtain advances of the amounts for the period involved and could mortgage parish property to obtain the necessary funds. A new structure of Poor Law Boards was created for each area to which Guardians would be elected triennially. Moreover, it was intended that Outdoor Relief would be extended to those in need, without reference to Parliament, for a period of two months, to be renewed when necessary.

The momentum for reform of the Poor Laws, much in evidence in Britain, carried over into Ireland at the beginning of the twentieth century. A Vice-Royal Commission was set up to enquire into the running of Poor Law Unions and to establish what changes were necessary to reduce their cost while maintaining their efficiency. The Commission reported in 1905, reiterating that enterprises which would provide employment for the able-bodied would increase the country's resources. Proposals to increase the range of facilities for the sick and elderly were also advanced.

A further report was received at Westminster in the same year from the Royal Commission on Poor Law and Relief of Distress. This report made recommendations of a radical nature. It recommended the abolition of the Boards of Guardians in Ireland and the transfer of responsibility for relief to local government bodies. It further recommended the breaking-up of services for the needy into special categories; the extension of Outdoor Relief to the able-bodied, including small landowners of over a quarter of an acre.

The Liberal Party won power in 1906 by an overwhelming vote on issues that rose from the way in which the poor were being treated. The new Government set about improving the living conditions of the poor with no little vigour. They introduced a series of Acts which were to form the basis of what was to become known later as the 'Welfare State'. These were the Old Age Pension Act 1908, the Labour Exchange Act 1909 and the National Insurance Act 1911. They were introduced into Ireland simultaneously and were supervised by Insurance Commissioners in Dublin.

The last two Acts had limited application to the working population, which was largely agricultural. In Northern Ireland 19.6 per cent were excluded from the provisions of the Acts for this reason, while the number of elderly qualified to receive the pension was substantially greater than elsewhere because of the age distribution of the Irish population. Therefore, the implementation of the Acts proved costly to the Exchequer because up to the war years, Irish contributions to the schemes did not meet the costs of running them.[12]

The most important change, however, resulted from government circulars in 1910 and 1911 to the Boards of Guardians indicating that a more compassionate attitude to the destitute and needy would be encouraged. The 1911 Order stated explicitly that the Boards could depart from any regulation to give adequate relief in any form provided that they received the approval of the Local Government Board.

These changes were consolidated later, though not in Ireland, in the efforts made by the Government to mobilise manpower in the First World War. Plainly, it was only possible to mobilise on such a large scale by introducing economic arrangements on egalitarian principles for soldiers' dependants. These arrangements were aimed at keeping up army morale and, for the first time, extending financial support as of right to those left behind as well as those fighting in the front line.

The method adopted was to by-pass the Guardians, who were still pre-occupied with reducing the local rates, and provide the money for relief purposes from government sources. After the war it reverted back to the rates which were quickly put under strain because of the return of large numbers of ex-soldiers to areas where considerable numbers of jobs were disappearing as the wartime economy was dismantled.

6

The Operation of the Poor Law in Belfast

When the new Government took over in Northern Ireland in 1921 the same structure of Poor Law Boards, Union Areas, workhouses and local rating systems was retained despite evidence contained in the Commissions' reports of 1905 and 1909 that there was a pressing need for reform. Both Commissions had underlined the fact that the Board of Guardians and the workhouse tests should have been replaced by more humane criteria. The content of the reports was ignored in Belfast. In the Free State, however, the new administration, in the light of what had been stated in the reports, abolished the Poor Law in 1924. The Unionist Government, on the other hand, recognising the importance of controlling the provision of social security to its population, kept it in operation. While the Poor Law had a soft form prior to 1920, when it was administered from Dublin, it had a hard and lethal form as well as a more sinister purpose afterwards.

The Unionists were now in power and the restraining hand of Dublin administrators was removed. The Poor Law Guardians, representatives of the Belfast bourgeoisie, had now a free hand in using the Poor Law system according to their own economic and social philosophy. Moreover they believed they were serving their class and defending their country from its enemies in the process.

It had always been clear to them that one function of the Poor Law Guardians was to exclude supporters of the political Opposition from relief, while aiding government supporters. They had been faithful to Unionist Party requirements in the past and it was assumed that they would be faithful in the future. Especially so, since survival of the new Government depended on them fulfilling their duty to the Party and its strategy.

Little change was envisaged under the new regime. Workhouse tests on destitution were rigidly applied by the administrators of the Board of Guardians who were already notorious for their puritanical parsimony long before 1920. Indeed these same Guardians were recognised by Catholic leaders as being the primary part of the apparatus for containing the numbers of their section of the Belfast population. After 1921 this function was intensified.

Around 1920, working-class people, who constituted the vast majority of the 400,000 citizens of Belfast, lived in 80,000 small houses set out in rows, back to back in 3,500 streets. These houses had been built by owners of local factories and were located in the inner area of the city. Factories to the north and west of the city processed flax and manufactured textiles; those to the east engaged in heavy engineering, including shipbuilding, while South Belfast provided homes for the slightly better-off from the service industries.

Many of the houses to the north, east and west had been built during the first part of the nineteenth century, and were of the most primitive type, consisting of a kitchen and a small scullery downstairs, with one bedroom and boxroom upstairs. Running water was supplied by a tap behind the front door. Gaslight, when the money was available for the penny 'meter', lighted the house. An open fire grate, which burned anything from sticks to coal, provided what heat and cooking was required. An outside lavatory, sometimes dry, served the four to six families that lived nearest the location and the sanitation, such as existed, assaulted the nostrils on approach.

Breadwinners and other members of their families fortunate enough to be employed earned little more than a pittance in working conditions which were so wretched that they were described in factory inspectors' annual reports as being the worst of any factory district in the British Isles.[1]

Except during the war when they were paid more, skilled engineers were paid an average of £2 per week; the unskilled males and females received proportionately less than that. In the mills, women, and children from the age of twelve upwards, worked six days a week for ten hours a day at sweated labour. Children were employed up to the early Twenties on a half-time basis – one day at school and the next in the mills and factories. Wages for the half-timers were paid at the rate of 2s. 9d. for a 58-hour fortnight. Because of the constant use of hot water, which was necessary to the flax processing, workers were compelled to toil in their bare feet in wet clothing throughout their working day. It was due to these working conditions that tuberculosis was rampant amongst Belfast workers.

Thomas Carnduff, the Belfast shipyard poet, referring to the period, stated in his unpublished memoirs that:

> spinners, especially if they were getting on in years, had to remain at work till they actually fell off their feet with exhaustion, or age made it impossible to carry on. One morning an aged woman employee slid to the floor of the factory and died quietly. She was carried into the storeroom on a wooden frame and laid there until the ambulance should arrive. I was detailed to keep the rats away from the body.

In the factories working conditions were so bad, particularly with dense impurities in the atmosphere, that factory inspectors calculated the life of a carder to be only seventeen years. Juvenile deaths in the fifteen-to-twenty age group in this industry were twice that of Manchester.

Outside workers who took material to make up on machines at home were paid at the rate of one penny per hour. Some employers even charged them for the thread! This practice to a large extent undermined the earning rates of factory workers and, to a lesser extent, those of the mill workers.

Saidie Patterson, a prominent Belfast trade unionist, speaking of this period said,

> It was my job to go to the warehouse to collect bundles of work and then, the following day, to return the finished goods. Mother was paid a pittance. I have her last pay packet. Wages 16s. 3d. for 50 dozens sheets and overalls less one shilling for thread.[2]

Infringements of the Factory Acts were in evidence everywhere. As there were too few factory inspectors to enforce the legislation, such infringements rarely reached the courts. Whenever they did, the Magistrates did not convict because of their sympathy with the employers. Hence the provisions contained in the Acts were disregarded and breaches of the Acts ignored.

Extreme poverty caused by a dramatic loss of jobs and falling wages in the aftermath of the war brought deep physical and mental stress to the residents of Belfast. Some parts were less affected than others. Some families were relieved from the effects of the depression by small injections of charity sent from abroad by family friends and relatives. Work in the engineering establishments was scarce. By the late Twenties, there were few jobs in the large factories and some of the shipyards showed signs of closing down.

The only jobs that were available in the textile and linen mills were provided for women. In families of North and West Belfast the bread-winner was usually the mother. Occasionally the father was offered night-shift work in the same mill at 27s. 6d. for a forty-eight-hour week. This rate was just slightly above that set for unemployment insurance. It was tolerable only to the unemployed because it enabled them, after a temporary period of employment, to qualify for benefit.

Throughout these years the signs of decay were everywhere. Housing stock became blighted; furniture deteriorated; family cloth-ing, repaired nightly, fell into tatters. Footwear on children was regarded at times as a provision of unnecessary comfort. Children with shaven heads, bare feet and rickets were commonplace in Belfast streets. The staple diet consisted of bread, potatoes and porridge; soup and rice were reserved for a religious feast day. A popular story in Belfast at the time was that William Gallagher, the Glasgow Commun-ist MP, when being driven around this area in an election brake, came upon some graffiti on the gable wall of a house. One slogan read, 'No Pope here', whereupon Gallagher was heard to mutter, 'Lucky Pope'.

For gala occasions, like Christmas and Easter, a piece of 'kitchen' was acquired to be served with the bread or cooked potatoes. (The term 'kitchen' was derived from what was prepared in the kitchens of the big houses where the upper classes lived – i.e. meat!)

Pawn shops, with three brass balls hung outside, were as numerous on the main streets as bookmakers' shops are at present. Items of value like suits, coats, boots and wedding rings were deposited for small loans that were needed to tide families over such occasions as weddings, wakes, births and illnesses. Until these items were redeemed interest on the loans was paid by clients at regular intervals to the pawnbroker. Indeed, I remember as a boy my mother 'pawning' her wedding ring for a half crown loan to pay a doctor after he had treated me for a lung infection. My aunt, who lived on her own and was receiving medicine from the local Poor Law dispensary, got me a bottle of cough mixture which was drawn from a large tank at the rear of the dispensary in Glengall Street. The mixture was believed to have universal curative powers. It was used for coughs, headaches, cuts, corns, bruises, and getting rid of lice. No household would be without several bottles of it. As children we always believed that this cough mixture tank was filled by a lorry using the same equipment that currently makes deliveries to petrol stations.

The society that the Unionist Government inherited was ideal for a political party like theirs to maintain its hegemony. The Poor Law system was worked on the basis that only by the means test for entry to the workhouse could relief be provided to the needy – who were mainly the people they considered to be in political opposition. The Government therefore had a vested interest in ignoring the calls for change of the system. They believed it affected only their political enemies whom they were already excluding from employment and from unemployment insurance. And they believed that if the enemies were further excluded from relief, they would be forced to face the grim choice of starving or emigrating.

To make the system operate in a politically selective way the Guardians needed an element of discretion in the interpretation of their statutory obligation to the poor. As a result the application of Outdoor Relief was never uniform. It varied from area to area and from time to time for no justifiable reason. Nevertheless in places like Newry, where the majority of the Guardians were Catholic, the Board was never allowed to apply the more generous sections of the Local Government (Ireland) Act 1898, even though the number of able-bodied destitute of the population was higher, pro rata, than in any other area of the North apart from Belfast.[3] It was offered to Belfast because the Government knew that it would be used to the advantage of their own supporters. Section 13 of the Local Government (Ireland) Act 1898 was more stringest in its use. It was therefore available to those Boards that were composed of Guardians opposed to the Unionist Government.

In other areas where the Poor Law Guardians were entirely Protestant, no difficulty was experienced by the Board in securing resources to meet the needs of all the able-bodied destitute on the occasions that they made application for relief.

The needy had no title to relief or financial help, for such a title or right to financial benefits would have lifted the pressure off the Catholic or anti-Unionist sections of the population. They would have felt less compulsion in that case to leave Northern Ireland. But selective denial of relief to Catholics increased the pressure on them. Indeed emigration from Catholic areas of Belfast was heaviest in the years that followed the pogrom of 1920.[4]

The formal transfer of power to the Belfast Board of Guardians took place on their receiving a letter from the Ministry of Home Affairs on

9 November 1921. A resolution was passed on 29 November in which the Guardians affirmed their intention of assisting and co-operating with the Government in ensuring an amicable and smooth-working arrangement. Henceforth, the Ministry of Home Affairs would sanction every job, appointment, grant and intake to workhouses in Northern Ireland.

In 1922 the Government Auditor, Mr G. Bryan, commenting on the financial report for the previous six months which showed an overall reduction of £6,281 in Poor Law payments but an increase in Outdoor Relief payments of £980, said that he allowed it to pass only with considerable hesitation. He admitted to having doubts about whether all the cases could be considered within the statute which authorised this form of relief. The chairman, in reply, said that matters were being stretched because they had taken into account the high number of unemployed and the temporary stoppage of grants to them, 'but that the amount spent weekly on Outdoor Relief had fallen from £160 in September last to £131 last week' and that he could predict 'a further reduction for this year's expenditure'.

It was clear from the Auditor's intervention that his authority was to be all-embracing and that he would apply conditions so stringently to the Board of Guardians' test of relief that only genuine destitute supporters of the Government would receive it. Bryan's stricture as early as this on the Poor Law Guardians was a signpost they could not ignore. Already their reputation was established for having the lowest rate amongst the major cities in the United Kingdom. It could be safely assumed, with this type of encouragement, that they would strive strenuously to improve on that reputation.

In Belfast, the Guardians were made up of thirty-four members elected from the local government wards, with additions from the greater Belfast area. Usually, around thirty of these members were Unionists, and were in constant contact with Unionist headquarters which had moved from the Old Town Hall in Belfast after the early Twenties to the present site in Glengall Street. They were located next door to the largest Poor Law dispensary, only several hundred yards away from the Belfast Union headquarters, the workhouse, the Belfast City Hall and the various Ministry offices of the Government. As a result, leading members of all these bodies congregated daily in the Unionist Party headquarters. The Guardians, petit bourgeois to a man, were understandably impressed with the aura of big business and high politics that permeated the building when they dropped in for a social chat each day. They fostered the friendships that developed with Government officials and Ministers. They had good reason so to do; there was always the possibility of picking up 'perks' or receiving patronage from the party machine. Dr John Oliver, Permanent Secretary of two major Stormont departments, described with relish in his memoirs the Minister of Home Affairs, Dawson Bates, MP, ringing up a friend in the motor trade to order tyres for the entire fleet of police vehicles.

Dawson Bates held the post of Unionist Party Secretary for many years before being appointed Minister of Home Affairs, which was the most powerful position in the Government after the Premiership. He had the Prime Minister's ear on all matters affecting Party organisation and was reported to run the Party from his office at Home Affairs. He encouraged the volume of social intercourse that took place around Unionist Party headquarters. This enabled him, on behalf of the Party, to maintain a certain amount of control of the affairs of local bodies such as the Belfast City Council, the Water Board and the Board of Guardians, and to make certain that jobs, salaried positions and public works' contracts were given to the party 'faithful'.

Elections for the Belfast Board of Guardians were held every three years on a limited voting register. The register allowed for multiple votes for members of the business community but deprived adult members of each household of the right to vote except in the case of the householder and his spouse. Predictably, each election for the Poor Law Guardians was a petit bourgeois triumph!

The Guardians were mainly drawn from petit bourgeoisie and reflected strongly the prejudices associated with that class. They were mainly Calvinistic in religious belief and believed paupers, destitute as well as able-bodied unemployed, were being punished by God for some sin they had committed. They also believed that the destitute were scheming constantly to steal money from the Belfast ratepayers by dishonestly misrepresenting their domestic circumstances when applying for relief, and, but for their great sagacity and vigilance in carrying out their duties as Guardians, the destitute of Belfast would steal from the rates on a grand scale.

Trades and professions of Poor Law Guardians named in the Belfast Street Directory are set out overleaf. Most of the information came from the Directory: the rest came from interviews with people still alive who were acquainted with the Guardians.

Occupation	1924	1932	1939
Housewives and others with private means	5	4	5
Estate Agents and Rate Collectors	2	1	1
Money Lenders/Pawnbrokers	1	1	–
Hospital Employees	2	1	1
Dentists/Doctors	1	1	1
Drapers	2	1	1
Furniture Removers and Undertakers	1	2	3
Catering Contractors	1	–	–
Photographers	1	1	–
Butchers	1	1	–
Coopers	1	1	1
Confectioners	1	–	–
Waste Merchants	1	–	–
Gas Meter Manufacturers	1	–	–
Small Cinema Owners	1	–	1
Publicans	1	3	1
Grocers	1	5	3
Brush Makers	1	1	1
Chemists	1	–	–
Headstone Sculptors	1	–	–
Garage Owners	1	–	–
Office Managers	1	2	3
Fitters	1	–	1
Builders' Suppliers	–	1	2
Manufacturers' Agents	–	4	5
Shoe Repairers	–	1	1
Architects	–	–	1
Hairdressers	–	–	1
Coal Merchants	–	–	1
	30	31	34

The Board of Guardians operated on a pyramid-like structure of small committees which reported to the Board for its weekly meeting when each set of minutes was adopted. The small committees met once or twice a month; the Outdoor Relief Committee, when required. They covered matters such as child welfare, finance, admissions, relieving officers' reports, workhouse affairs, requisition and purchasing, medical reports as well as correspondence. The Board met on each appointed Tueday at noon in the office of the Belfast Union. The Union Jack flew overhead while the Board was in session.

Poor Law administration in Belfast was well known for its inhumanity to the destitute. Evidence of this was regularly demonstrated at Outdoor Relief meetings where applicants were required to attend in person for interview. No subject was sacred. No question, no matter how personal, was ruled out. Detailed information was asked for on the applicants' private life and discussed cynically by the Board. Often Catholics were told to ignore Church teachings on sex. The same attitude rubbed off on the Board's employees in the dispensaries where the relieving officers issued grocery chits and mass-produced medicines. Often applicants reacted so bitterly to this treatment that railings had to be erected to protect relieving officers and their staff from physical abuse.

One Chairman of the Outdoor Relief committee in the early Thirties, Mrs Lily Coleman, is still remembered in the Catholic ghettoes for an observation she was wont to make to applicants with large families that 'there was no poverty under the blankets'. This quote was used extensively as a slogan by the strikers in the 1932 riots.

The Guardians' prejudices against the Catholic destitute were shown on a regular basis in their Minutes. They pointed out on a number of occasions that 60 per cent of those applying for relief had been encourged to get as much as they could from the rates while receiving relief from Catholic charities.

The latter part of this statement was untrue as a cursory examination of the facts could have shown. Catholic charities extended no relief to the Catholic destitute except in cases where relief was refused by the statutory authorities. They were forced to step in only when the Poor Law Guardians had refused to meet their obligations to the Belfast poor.

One Guardian, recorded in the Poor Law Minutes of 8 August 1928, gave his version of the Guardians' obligation to the poor:

> Faced with such sloth, fecklessness and iniquity, the Guardians' duty was to discourage idleness and to create a spirit of independence since much of the money given to the poor was wasted...He knew of three betting shops in one street which did a roaring business amongst the poor... These people would make an effort to find work if they found that they could not get relief.

The reference was to a Catholic area. On the whole, Catholic businessmen in Belfast invested only in public houses and betting shops. It was only until recently religious considerations tended to inhibit Protestants from trading in these businesses.

Relieving officers' reports, drafted after the applicant's initial visit, were crucial to each case. They were compiled to establish intimate information on each application which included the religion, family origins and blood relations. It was essential to the Unionist strategy to identify the religion of the applicant to enable the relieving officer to recommend for relief or to write out a chit for a job for the 'right' person whenever employment became available.[5]

Relief awards made to the destitute in the early Twenties were always in two, four, six and eight week segments. Relief was given in kind but not in money to the head of the household. It took no account of the need to pay rent, heat a house or to buy clothes. The items of food to be bought were printed on the back of the relief chit. This was called a 'Grocery Chit' and could only be used in a shop appointed for the area in which it was issued. It was invariably for a Unionist-owned shop. No other item of food could be obtained. Names of recipients were posted on gable walls nearest the home in an attempt to humiliate and deter those seeking relief. Relief in kind was granted in allowances ranging from a minimum of 6s. per week to a maximum of 25s. Applications for relief were always successful when accompanied by a letter from Unionist Headquarters. Relieving officers had authority to make small holding payments until cases were given consideration by the Board at its weekly meetings. But temporary payments, with all other awards, were entered in the Minutes and duly reported to the Minister of Home Affairs for sanction.[6]

Relieving officers as a rule behaved like petty tyrants towards applicants. They saw themselves as front-line soldiers in the campaign to force unwanted citizens of Belfast to move abroad, and they found the means as well as creating the will for these families to go. The will was created by putting pressure on applicants to sell everything of domestic value, including necessary pieces of furniture, to keep themselves. Relatives were approached and sometimes threatened with court proceedings unless they would maintain the able-bodied employed. Finally, fares to enable the destitute to emigrate were offered on terms that were almost impossible to refuse.

There were exceptions to this rule, of course. I was told the story of one humane, relieving officer who attended church each Sunday evening in the dock area. Local poor, faced with a new birth, a funeral in the family or some similar contingency, used to meet him coming out of church and found him usually amenable to their request for relief while he was in the state of grace.[7]

Few records of statistics are available from Northern Ireland Government sources to cover the period from 1920 to 1922. Those that are available do not reflect with accuracy the enormous volume of need that existed because of the social upheaval that folowed the Belfast riots of the early Twenties, and the severe economic depression which caused considerable contraction in traditional industries like shipbuilding and linen.

The numbers suffering from the effects of grinding poverty at the time were greater than those found in the earlier institutional records. The density of this problem is highlighted by the amount of work done by charitable associations of which approximately 200 were giving relief of some form to the destitute in the Belfast area. These associations administered relief on an ad hoc basis. Most of them were based on local or workplace organisations which gave help on a very meagre scale to the distressed in cash or kind. The more important of these, however, were the ones which covered large areas, had more resources, and were invariably rooted in religious societies.

In the wake of the bitter civil disturbances of 1920 when thousands of Catholics suffered the loss of their homes and expulsion from jobs, a number of charity funds were set up to collect monies to help combat hardship. Money was sent to Belfast from the South of Ireland, Canada, America and Australia. Almost £½ million was received and dispensed by two organisations – the Catholic Expelled Workers' Fund and the American White Cross Fund. Married men received £1 per week and single men 10s. The former organisation operated until 1922 and the latter until 1924, and were finally taken over by the Catholic Bishop of Down and Connor because of certain accounting 'discrepancies' which arose. The residue of the funds was put to use afterwards through the agency of the St Vincent de Paul Society to ameliorate the plight of the Catholic destitute in Belfast.[8]

These funds became the mainstay of support for the Catholic poor during the period 1920–24 and at various times afterwards. However ill the effects of the pogrom and the subsequent persecution of Catholics in Belfast, it would have been infinitely worse without these charity funds and the co-ordinated efforts of the St Vincent de Paul Society. Throughout the first four years of the Twenties this organisation was relieving more than eight people for every able-bodied person relieved by the Guardians through Outdoor Relief.

Relief granted by the St Vincent de Paul Society as compared with the number of people assisted by the Poor Law Board in Belfast and the Poor Law Board throughout Northern Ireland, extracted from the minute books of both organisations, is detailed below.

Number of people given relief during the years 1920–40

Year	St Vincent de Paul	Belfast Poor Law	N. Ireland Poor Law
1920	7,697	794	–
1921	12,710	1,052	–
1922	9,953	913	4,726
1923	9,765	1,005	4,884
1924	–	1,531	4,906
1925	8,613	1,821	5,365
1926	10,951	4,087	5,634
1927	13,690	6,446	7,564
1928	11,801	997*	9,286
1929	8,825	2,195	5,542
1930	7,371	1,379	6,321
1931	9,117	4,165	6,029
1932	9,558	14,345	9,602
1933	7,823	21,387	22,396
1934	7,117	20,127	30,557
1935	8,725	15,486	30,102
1936	8,418	12,306	26,099
1937	6,858	4,967	22,059
1938	8,220	6,326	13,993
1939	6,348	7,183	15,089
1940	7,516	5,510	45,598

*This figure reflects the action taken in 1928 by the Belfast Guardians in refusing relief to able-bodied unemployed.

The efforts of the St Vincent de Paul Society to help the Catholic destitute of Belfast were remarkable by any standard. They helped on average 9,500 people and spent £12,150 per annum over a period of twenty years. As can be seen by comparative figures it was not until 1932 that the efforts of the Poor Law Guardians to relieve the destitute in Belfast caught up with those of the Society.

This work by the St Vincent de Paul Society was carried out by twenty 'conferences' or parish units organised by voluntary workers in the Belfast area. Each parish unit collected from within its congregation the resources required to meet the needs of its destitute. When outlay was greater than its collections, the deficit was made up by the central organisation out of reserves.

Relief work by the St Vincent de Paul Society took various forms but was usually given in kind. Special homes were set up for industrial training, for the deaf and dumb and for orphans. The scope of help however, was not confined to that framework alone. Free meals for the destitute were provided daily; cast-off footwear and clothing were collected and distributed; and a small factory was opened to make disinfectants and firewood which were given out at nominal cost to poor families for re-sale on the doorstep. Quite often cash grants were given to pay rent or fares to enable families to emigrate.

In an effort to bring the troubles in Belfast to an end, Michael Collins, a leading member of the Irish Government, and James Craig met in the summer of 1921 and agreed a formula to bring peace to Northern Ireland. One of the recommendations made in the agreement and approved by the Westminster Government was for £500,000 to be provided to finance a number of public works projects. The money was to fund 50 per cent of the wage bill for 6,000 workers who would be drawn from all sections of the community. The Unionist Government made no effort to conform to their side of the agreement and commenced to use the £500,000 to provide employment for their own unemployed supporters.

Joseph Devlin, Catholic MP for West Belfast, raised the matter at Westminster on 14 June 1922 and criticised the spending of money on relief schemes which employed only Protestants. The Colonial Secretary, Winston Churchill, MP, already alerted in private by Devlin, replied that a senior civil servant, Mr S.G. Tallents, would be sent to Belfast to investigate the charges. The Unionist Government, and Craig in particular, were already under heavy censure from Churchill's Irish Committee, of which Tallents was a member, for the failure to adhere to the agreement made between Craig and Collins to end the persecution of Catholics in Northern Ireland. Churchill was strongly suspicious that the Unionists were working to a plan to clear Catholics out of Northern Ireland and for that reason Tallents was given a wider remit than that defined by Churchill in Parliament.

Tallents arrived in Belfast in June 1922 and immediately engaged in talks with a number of people, including the Catholic Bishops, on a wide range of issues. (He described Bates in a subsequent letter to his

Minister as a 'political hack' and his chief assistants as 'violent partisans'.)

Shortly after Tallents' visit the British Government announced that all relief schemes subsidised from their funds must employ a ratio of one Catholic to every two Protestants. The mechanics of a just system of recruitment of labour were evolved. A green card was given to each unemployed man which could be taken to a site foreman who would arrange a job for the bearer.

This new·scheme led to angry protests by Unionist politicians in Parliament, in the City Council and at the Poor Law Board. Government Ministers spoke out in public against the interference by Westminster. The relief scheme slowed down and gradually came to a halt. By 1925, when the Colwyn Committee presented its first report, it stated that only £300,000 had been drawn from the fund and no further drawings from it were contemplated. Clearly the employment of Catholics on public works projects did not conform to the objects of the Unionist strategy. They had no further use for the scheme in that form.

The Belfast Harbour Commissioners, totally committed to the Unionist strategy, though engaged at the time on a large-scale development programme for the Harbour Estate, refused to accept capital from the fund because of the requirement to employ a quota of Catholics in their labour force. No Catholics were employed there and they did not propose to create a precedent.

Perhaps the final word on the issue was expressed by the Minister of Labour who wrote to the Guardians on 10 November 1923, asking them to stop foremen and gangers informing the unemployed that they could get green cards for unemployment at the local Labour Exchange.[9]

Meanwhile, in the face of increasing poverty and the acute distress of most of the urban areas in Britain, public protests and demonstrations were taking place. Thirty Guardians in the Poplar district of London, led by George Lansbury, went to prison for insisting on paying people on Outdoor Relief above the pitiful scales fixed by the Government. Having gained control of the Council in 1919, Labour councillors found themselves in one of the most destitute boroughs in London, administering a rating system which the Mayor, George Lansbury, described as the poor helping the poor.

Outdoor Relief Scales, 1922

	Mond Scale (including winter fuel allowance of 3s. 0d. a week)	Poplar Scale (including winter fuel allowance of 3s. 0d. a week & rent allowance based on actual rent up to 10s. 0d.)
Man and wife	28s. 0d.	38s. 0d.
with 1 child	34s. 0d.	39s. 6d.
2 children	39s. 0d.	44s. 6d.
3 children	44s. 0d.	49s. 6d.
4 children	48s. 0d.	54s. 0d.
5 children	54s. 0d.	59s. 6d.
6 children	54s. 0d.	64s. 6d.
7 children	54s. 0d.	69s. 6d.
8 children	54s. 0d.	74s. 6d.

The Mond Scale was introduced by Sir Alfred Mond, in October 1921, after widespread pressure throughout the country, led by Poplar, for increased rates of relief. Of the twenty-seven Poor Law Boards in the London area, fifteen operated a lower scale than the new Mond Scale, eight revised theirs to come into line with it and four, including Poplar, operated a higher scale.

The message was picked up in Belfast. The minutes of the Poor Law Guardians for September 1921 indicated that a gradual build-up of pressure to improve the provision of relief was being mounted by the trade union movement. A delegation representing the workers of the Irish Textile Federation arrived at the workhouse while the Guardians were meeting on 9 September and were refused a hearing. The delegation consisted of Alderman Sam Kyle, Councillor Dawson Gordon, Miss Galway – a legendary figure in the trade union movement – and Harry Midgley. (Kyle and Midgley were elected later to the Northern Ireland Parliament.) The Belfast Trade Union Council, on hearing of the refusal to meet the delegation, issued a strong protest which may have had a bearing on the Guardians' convening a special meeting on 22 September on the matter. Nothing came from the meeting.

Pressure on the Guardians to meet the trade unions continued to mount, until finally the Board was forced to meet a delegation from the Amalgamated Engineering Union on 1 March 1922. Three members of the Union attended and were allowed to speak. Mr Courtney, who had led the delegation, said that out of a Belfast membership of 7,000, 1,505 were unemployed for one year and eight months and that it would be at least another two years before a return to normal working would take place.

Benefit at the labour exchange was only 15s. for a male, 5s. for a wife, and 1s. for a child, but Mr Courtney pointed out that his members had already run out of benefit. In Scotland steps had been taken to relieve able-bodied persons, but not in Belfast, although it was the same law as operated here. Mr Bell, another member of the delegation, said his members were in a critical condition, and had been waiting six weeks for additional benefit, but they would not allow their children to starve.[10]

The Chairman, in reply, said that all cases would be dealt with sympathetically, that he was a good business man and that the Vice-Chairman, a lady, might be regarded as sympathetic; that the Board had no indication of exceptional distress in the city; and that when the time came he was satisfied the Board would rise to the occasion. He had read last Saturday that the outlook was brighter and he gathered from that, that Belfast was about to go ahead again. The delegation withdrew and the minute stated baldly that the matter be 'dropped'.

In 1922 the Minister of Labour in the Northern Ireland Parliament introduced a Bill to amalgamate unemployment benefit and unemployment insurance into one measure similar to that which was being enacted in Britain at the same time. The Act enabled benefit of £1 per week to be paid to married men with an additional 1s. per child; 15s. for single men and 12s. for single women. The benefits would be paid out in periods of five weeks over a period of thirty weeks followed by three periods of five weeks in which nothing would be paid. The Minister of Labour was given power in the Act to grant an extension of two five-week periods if he felt it would be in the public interest.[11]

Throughout 1923, public protests against the Guardians and their policies were growing bigger and becoming more frequent. These protests, which were organised by unemployed workers, were providing a suitable opportunity for the labour leadership to return to public platforms without being subject to attack by Unionist mobs.

To avoid the growing threat from the unemployed, the Guardians decided on 11 December 1923 to seek authorisation to grant relief to heads of families ordinarily resident in the Belfast Union District who, for legitimate reasons, were not in receipt of unemployment or other state benefit. Unemployment was high and the Unionist Government was anxious to avoid the agitation created by militants across the water. Many skilled workers were amongst the unemployed – the Guardians had to recognise that fact.

The Guardians' resolution was passed to the Belfast Corporation to be referred formally to the Minister of Home Affairs, thus enabling them to administer relief outside the workhouse. This move constituted the most substantial departure from the destitution test since it was introduced in 1838.

However, the Ministry had no intention of condoning such departures from a policy of such political value to them. They countered on 24 December 1923, with a letter to the effect that relief in cases of exceptional distress could be met by putting into operation Section 13 of the Local Government Act 1898 with suitable safeguards by the Guardians themselves.

This was the first time that Section 13 of the 1898 Act was ever recommended or used in Northern Ireland to help the able-bodied unemployed, and it was to be a constant feature of the Board's activities from 2 February 1924, onwards. This section enabled the Guardians to grant relief outside the workhouse for any time not exceeding two months from the date of the Order to poor persons of any description resident within that part of the Union which was situated within the Belfast County Borough subsequent to certain prescribed conditions: ie,

1. Relief given under the authority of this Order would be given at the Guardians' discretion to such persons being the heads of families ordinarily resident in any of the said electoral divisions, who for reasons satisfactory to the Guardians are not in receipt of or entitled to unemployment or any other state benefit, and who are unable to obtain employment.

2. Such relief shall only be given after full enquiry into the circumstances of each case, and shall be in the form in which the Outdoor Relief is usually given by the Guardians to persons eligible for such under Section 1 of the Poor Relief Extension Act 1847.

3. If, after consideration of any case, the Guardians consider it desirable they may offer Indoor Relief notwithstanding that Outdoor Relief might be granted under the Order.

The Guardians were also authorised to appoint, subject to the Ministry's approval, so many temporary relieving officers as would be found necessary to the effective administration of such relief. The unemployed were not impressed by the decision of the Guardians to offer temporary relief over a slightly longer period, while refusing to increase the measure of relief.

The Government recognised the long-term implications of the unemployment problem. The traditional industries were rapidly contracting. There were too few jobs available. Their own supporters were being forced out of work for extended periods. Unemployment benefit could only be paid out for a limited period; something else was required to keep unemployed workers who were supporters of the Government until the economy improved. Outdoor Relief was an ideal instrument for the Unionists in that it could be applied without inflexible statutory control of its use. Information of a personal nature could disclose to the Guardians the political tendencies of the applicant, who would receive relief for any period that the Outdoor Relief Committee determined as long as they believed him to be a Government supporter. Applicants who were not Government supporters were refused relief.

In England, the large number of new Labour Guardians elected in post-war elections were beginning to establish an effective presence on Boards throughout the country. Through sheer weight of numbers, these Guardians were making certain that everyone applying for relief was assured of sufficient clothing, food and housing. The rule that men had to work for relief was ignored. Boards upon which the Labour Guardians were in a minority were from 1924 onwards subject to sharp and growing protest from organisations like the National Unemployed Workers Movement. The campaign to help the poor was widespread and not confined to the efforts of the Poor Law Guardians. The Labour Government, in office with the help of a Liberal vote, used public pressure to improve pensions and unemployment benefits.

In Belfast, however this was not the case. *The Labour Opposition,* a monthly periodical issued by the Independent Labour Party, in March 1925 carried an editorial denouncing the Unionist Government for interfering with the increases to cash benefits granted by the Ramsay

McDonald Government to old age pensioners and the unemployed. The Government of Northern Ireland attempted to impose conditions on the payment of increases so that they would be paid only at the will and discretion of the Minister.[12] This was just another example of departing from parity in social security when it did not conform to strategic requirements.

On 19 January 1924, 4,000 unemployed arrived to protest outside the Poor Law Guardians' meeting and were left standing in the road-way. Only twelve were allowed into the workhouse, two of whom entered the boardroom to address the Guardians. Alderman Kyle, one of those received in the boardroom, appealed on the grounds of common justice for 24s. per week unemployment benefit to be paid and to do away with the 'gap' weeks. He estimated that another £10,000 a year would cover the extra costs and would put only one penny on the rates.[13]

The Chairman of the Committee, Mr John Wilson, JP, replied that he had received a 'death warrant' that morning. He commenced to read a long and detailed statement, in which he claimed that the unemployed workers' demand would cost the tax-payers £781,948, or an extra 10s. in the pound on the rates. He said that there would be no incentive to men to work if they could get these increased grants. It would be a disastrous policy to pursue, he said, if unemployed workers honestly desiring work and unable to find it should be thrown on Poor Law for a means of livelihood. Wilson's speech was reported so fully in the minutes that it was patently obvious that the Clerk of the Board had written it for him. The speech was written into the Board's minutes in detail, which was unusual; the important parts were emphasised by the Clerk using capital letters. The demonstration went to the wrong place. Since it was unemployment benefit they wished to improve they should have gone to the Ministry of Labour. In any case Kyle's figures were right and Wilson's wildly wrong.

The same day, in total disregard of Wilson's speech, the Ministry of Home Affairs made an Order, under the Local Government Act, authorising the Board of Guardians to administer relief outside the workhouse for two months. This order was to be repeated at two-monthly intervals until 1927, because of constant and unremitting pressure by the unemployed workers, the trade unions and to some extent by the British Legion.

At the Poor Law elections in June of that year, the labour move-ment, breaking the Unionist stranglehold, elected two of its most

91

notable and aggressive representatives, William McMullen and Jack Beattie. Both were trade union leaders and fierce critics of the Poor Law system.

At their first meeting, the Chairman refused Beattie the right of reply to a motion which he had earlier moved. Beattie, a blacksmith by trade, refused physically to let anyone else speak. He was backed up by McMullen, no less determined and a formidable figure in his own right. The meeting was quickly brought to an end. This proved to be a harbinger for the future. Police were present at each meeting afterwards.

Dawson Bates recognised the significance of the election of the labour representatives to the Board of Guardians. He knew that if the Guardians were left to their own instincts they would force their callous treatment of the destitute to the forefront of political life – thus providing the right issue for the labour movement to make a comeback in local elections. To save the Guardians from their own excesses he put forward, on 7 April 1924, a proposal to set up a departmental committee to enquire into local government administration which would include the Poor Law in Northern Ireland. The committee was instructed:

1. to enquire into the allocation amongst local authorities and local committees of their different powers and duties in connection with local government, public health, poor law and allied services

2. to enquire as to their suitability and efficiency

3. to enquire into the costs and to recommend alternatives in the allocation of such powers and duties.[14]

The enquiry was little more than a token gesture towards the Guardians' activities in the hope of placating the political Opposition. But the Guardians by this time were so full of their own puritanical zeal for punishing those sinners, that the overall strategy of subtle discrimination against Opposition supporters for political reasons was entirely lost on them. The Guardians were bent on inflicting punishment on the destitute, Protestant and Catholic alike. The Government knew that this bloody-mindedness would cost them dearly in succeeding elections. They had two options – they could curb the Guardians' powers, especially on the matter of discretion, or alternatively, they could allow the Guardians to carry on with full powers of discretion as to whom should be helped, but keep pressure on them through the party machine to make certain that those they were helping wore the right party colours. They decided on the latter course.

Bates knew what was required of him by the Party and made no real effort to reform the Poor Law system. The criticisms of the Commission's reports, which had been submitted earlier to the Liberal Government at Westminster, were still relevant and could have been acted upon with immediate effect if Bates had so desired. He wanted no change in the system: for the Unionist Government, its inadequacies were its strength in that they could be used, providing the users abided by Party directions, to carry out the Government's strategic requirements. Party directives given privately to the Guardians were that they should use their power to keep Government supporters relieved from poverty between jobs while aggravating the destitution of Opposition supporters.

7

The Guardians Kick Over the Traces

By 1924 serious problems were developing in relation to the administration of the Belfast Poor Law. Because of their almost fanatical prejudices against the destitute, the Poor Law Guardians were alienating not only Catholics but a large number of the able-bodied unemployed who were Protestant.

The Unionist Government had never been the natural friend of the poor in the way that a Labour administration like that of Ramsay McDonald had been. But the members of a Unionist Government had enough sense in these matters to conceal where their real sympathies lay in a way that the members of the Board refused to do. The Guardians' public behaviour, in the future as in the past, was to become a deepening source of embarrassment to the Government as well as the cause of bitter resentment among the Belfast poor.

The Guardians were unable to restrain their 'moral' feelings against supporting paupers. And they believed that it was an act of patriotism on their part not to support 'spongers' and malingerers who did not want to work. After all, were they not elected by the petit-bourgeoisie to keep the rates down? Did not the low rates of relief paid out by them have a bearing on wages paid by local employers, enabling them to compete effectively with businesses elsewhere, especially against those from the South of Ireland? Was not this service to employers also a service to their country in its hour of need? This mentality which had been latent before 1920 became the ideology once the Unionists came to power. The Guardians, conscious of their own importance to the strategy, were to put their own punitive mark on how the Poor Law system would work.

By 1925 a certain amount of public resentment already existed against the Guardians because relief and benefit scales to the able-bodied unemployed were known to be less than those granted in Britain. In major British cities public protests and popular demonstrations had been the order of the day since 1919. While they may not have been too successful at Westminster they certainly loosened the purse strings at local level where the English Poor Law Guardians, unlike those in Belfast, were subject to a fair and regular test at the ballot box – a test that forced the English Guardians to conform to civilised standards of administration. Nevertheless, demonstrations against Poor Law policies did occur in Belfast when large numbers of applicants were refused relief after being taken off extended unemployment benefit, on the spurious grounds that the unemployed were not making reasonable efforts to secure work.

Sam Kyle, who had been elected to Parliament a short time before, with Jack Beattie and William McMullen, spoke on the matter in an unemployment debate. Referring to men who were turned down for this reason he reported that he had witnessed them being batoned by police while fighting amongst themselves that morning in an attempt to get a foreman to give them a job on public work schemes. These were the same men who allegedly were not making reasonable efforts to secure work.

On 6 October 1925, a march to the workhouse, planned to coincide with the holding of a Board meeting, was banned by the Minister of Home Affairs under the Special Powers Act 1921. This legislation had been enacted in the first days of the Northern Ireland Parliament to combat the activities of the IRA. It was used on this occasion, as it was to be used on other occasions in the future, to stop the poor from complaining in public about physical hardship and the misery of their existence.

Beattie and McMullen were constantly active in the Guardians' boardroom on behalf of the Belfast poor. Through the whole of 1924 until they were both elected to Parliament in 1925, they raised a number of pertinent issues in a most impertinent way.[1]

They insisted that all relief should be paid in cash, along parallel lines with payments made in England; that no Poor Law officials or employees should be released with pay to work for Unionist Party members in future elections; and that the 'B' Special Police Force should not be permitted to use the workhouse grounds for firing practice as it frightened the inmates.[2]

The Labour MPs, keeping up their attack in the Northern Ireland Parliament, were soon joined by Joe Devlin, a Westminster MP who seemed impressed by their effectiveness in the debating chamber. He and his party colleagues had boycotted Parliament since 1921 because

95

of their feelings of hopelessness in the face of an authoritarian Unionist regime. Labour's performance gave Devlin hope that the Northern Ireland Parliament would begin to work like Westminster.

The Labour MPs were a formidable trio. They formed the nucleus of an effective Opposition when they were joined by the Nationalist, Joe Devlin, and Tom Henderson, an Independent Unionist. They opened debates in the House on pressing social and economic matters that were comparable in quality if not in scale with those taking place at Westminster on similar issues. Ministers for the first time were kept on their toes defending the operations of their departments. Briefs were padded out to ward off intelligent and well-informed supplementary questions. The Prime Minister was sent for regularly to save the Government's face, particularly against Devlin, known as the 'pocket Demosthenes' because of his debating skills at Westminster.

The number receiving Outdoor Relief increased from 3,345 on 20 December 1925, to 4,657 on 12 January 1926. McMullen, detecting a reduction in relief payments proposed an increase in the scale of relief at the meeting of the Belfast Guardians in January 1926. He, with another member of the Board, was ruled out of order for criticising policy. Police were called and four members, including McMullen and Beattie, were thrown out bodily amongst the crowd of protesters who had gathered outside the gates.

On 31 March 1926, a recommendation from the Outdoor Relief Committee to grant a single man living on his own 6s. per week was amended to allow for an increase of 4s. to Boer War veterans. The mover of the amendment said that Catholics in West Belfast got the 'bad end of the stick' and had been denied the right to work since 1920. The chairman replied, in opposing the amendment, that Catholics were disinclined to work.[3]

Several months later, the Unemployed Workers' Organisation, which by now had commenced to organise in Belfast, wrote a letter asking that a delegation of members be received on 12 May to urge on the Guardians the necessity of keeping grants on the same level as those paid by Boards in Great Britain. Standing Orders were suspended for the occasion and the delegation, led by an influential craft trade union official named Sam Geddis, was admitted to address the Board. Geddis, admitting that he was a government appointment to the Unemployment Committee for Northern Ireland, said that the live register for unemployed in Belfast on 3 May was 29,938; his

Unemployment Rota Committee had held 88 meetings in one month, dealing with 12,467 claims, 9,667 of which were approved, 1,938 rejected and not receiving unemployment benefit, and 2,800 struck off the register. Geddis felt that the latter numbers would repeat themselves each month from then on because exception would be taken to those who were: 1, not normally on insurable employment; 2, not making reasonable efforts to find work; 3, not having had a reasonable period of employment last time around; and 4, not likely to obtain unsurable employment again.

In addition, he said that his delegation had seen the Minister of Home Affairs before coming to the Guardians – the reason no doubt for their prompt reception. The Minister, he said, had assured them that the Guardians had enough powers to deal with destitution. If they had not then he would give them more.[4] (Geddis represented those union interests that supported the Government throughout the early Twenties.) The response to the delegation at the meeting was a negative one, though Geddis' speech was well-informed and merited response by the Guardians. Even with the Minister's imprimatur, they were turned away. The true colours of the Unionist Guardians were displayed several weeks later when Mrs Lily Coleman proposed that all cases being considered that day be turned down as they had too many to determine. Newspaper reports published on 27 May state that McMullen and Beattie had to be physically restrained by other Guardians in their reaction to this proposal.

Meanwhile at Stormont the matter was being ventilated by the Labour MPs who tried to push the Government into accepting provision for the needy as a national obligation and grants for the relief of the poor to be paid at the same rates as those given to the unemployed in Britain. This debate led to a letter being sent by the Minister of Home Affairs to the Guardians concerning exceptional distress in the Belfast area. Beattie remarked in public that he hoped 'the unemployed would march up to the workhouse and throw the Guardians out'.[5]

He seemed to be expressing the views of a great many people *vis-a-vis* the uselessness of the Guardians to the Belfast poor. He was more fortunate than Samuel Patterson of Wyndham Street, who had no parliamentary protection and had to face a charge of having made a seditious speech about the Guardians on 14 June 1926, on the Shankill Road. The Crown Solicitor said in court the following day that Patterson was endeavouring to incite certain persons to acts of crime and to prevent by force of arms an execution of the law of the realm. He was sentenced subsequently to six months' imprisonment.

Patterson was chairman of a meeting of 100 people and was quoting scripture for them when the police charged the crowd and arrested him.

'Comrades and unemployed', he was saying, 'we read in the Scriptures that the earth is the Lord's and the fullness thereof. We are here to bring to your notice the demonstration of the unemployed that is to take place tomorrow to the Poor Law Guardians... Demonstrations are no good... you were heroes when you were in the trenches. If you were still the same heroes, 300 of you could still go up to the work-house, even though you have not the privilege of having a six-pounder behind you and take possession for a day. You could compel the dirty boss class to grant your demands. If you do not back up the miners, by force if necessary, you will be like them if they are beaten, chained in bundles by this damnable system we are compelled to live in. Here are the police coming. They are always on the alert when revolution is spoken of. Run like hell!'[6]

The following day a large party of the unemployed, led by a number of bands, arrived outside the workhouse after walking from the City Hall. A large force of police was there to meet them. A delegation which had been appointed earlier was refused admission. The two Labour MPs arrived at the gates and after addressing the crowd, they entered the boardroom for the meeting. They immediately obstructed the business of the meeting when they realised that it did not refer to the matter of Outdoor Relief. They were seized by the police and dumped outside the workhouse, on the pavement of the Lisburn Road.[7]

Philip Wilson, another Labour Guardian, speaking to the crowd gathered outside the workhouse gates, pointed out that £5,000 was paid out each week in Camberwell to 4,335 people, while £575 7s.2d. was paid out in Belfast to 4,623 people.

Whatever their view of the Guardians, it was clear that the Government was not prepared to tolerate any public demonstrations against them. In Parliament, Sam Kyle raised the issue at Question Time on 6 October 1926. He insisted that the police had behaved in an excessively violent way and used abusive language when they removed his two Parliamentary colleagues from the Poor Law boardroom. The Minister, Dawson Bates, replied that the chairman of a local authority had common law powers to direct the removal by force of anyone who did not obey his ruling. Mr S.B. Hanna, KC, Parliamentary Secretary, went even further when he said that the Labour members were making a big mistake if they thought they could hold public meetings and preach sedition!

This incident, the Minister's Parliamentary Secretary's remarks in the debate, as well as the spontaneous use made of the Special Powers Act, must have reinforced the determination of the Guardians in the exercise of their duties. Events in England at this time were having a bearing on their attitude to the increased number of applicants for relief – especially the punitive effect of government policies on the unemployed after the failure of the General Strike. Clearly the Guardians were being encouraged by the Government to refuse relief except in cases where the male parent was prepared to subject himself to the indignity of living in the workhouse.

What encouraged the Belfast Guardians even more was the modification to the system of relief grants which was introduced by some Poor Law Boards, to compel recipients to go through a form of rehabilitation or training. Chamberlain's Board of Guardians (Default) Act, which was passed in 1926, created the right atmosphere for them and they were further encouraged by the suspension of elected representatives in Westham, Chester-le-Street and Bedwelty for their liberal attitude to the relief of long-term unemployed in their areas.

The situation in England in 1926 was by no means the same as that which obtained in Belfast. Only 34 out of 631 Poor Law Unions were seriously affected, but not in the same chronic way as was Belfast. The vast majority of these Unions levied only a few pence in the pound to meet Poor Law charges, while others, with long-term unemployed, had to find as much as 20s. in the pound.[8]

However, by July 1927 the Belfast Guardians were pushing vigorously towards the establishment of a labour test before relieving able-bodied men. Their annual expenditure on Outdoor Relief under the Local Government Act 1898, which did not permit them to exceed three pence in the pound, gave them the opportunity. It was by now in excess of £42,000 per annum which represented 3d. in the pound rateable valuation. This gave the chairman of the Board an excuse to ask for legal opinion on the amount of money spent on relief, as against the legal restraint contained in the Act.[9]

At a Board meeting on 13 September the Chairman stated that the time had arrived when Indoor Relief should be granted only to those cases where they were satisfied that the legislative conditions were met. They believed as well that the Minister of Labour should be required to relieve all other classes of able-bodied persons.

Labour tests had been tried on a large number of occasions in England since the concept of Poor Law Relief had been introduced in the 1830s. It had never been successful because those tested were destitute lacking strength and scarcely competent workers. Employers favoured strong and competent workers, of which they was always an ample supply. In England the destitute in any case had the legal right to relief at the workhouse.[10] In Belfast, if a labour test was imposed, the able-bodied unemployed had no legal right to enter the workhouse. They had to work or starve. The Guardians therefore saw the introduction of a labour test as another weapon in their arsenal to help promote the strategic objectives of the Unionist Party.

If the Guardians had a peaceful passage for their proposals at Board meetings, their colleagues in Parliament were enjoying no such tranquility. Former Guardians McMullen and Beattie had joined up with Sam Kyle and Joe Devlin to launch a series of attacks on the Ministries of Home Affairs and Labour because of their refusal to stand up to the Belfast Guardians. Kyle and Devlin both admonished them for abolishing the Tyrone and Fermanagh Board of Guardians because it had ignored the Ministry's directive on granting extra relief payments, while tolerating the Belfast Board for refusing to carry out its statutory duty to the poor.[11]

The main attack came in the form of a motion of censure on the Minister of Home Affairs for giving in to the Belfast Guardians on the labour test. The MPs claimed that the labour test changed the nature of the relief granted and entitled the able-bodied unemployed to cash payments instead of relief in kind in contravention of the Truck Act. They were of the opinion that the workers employed under the labour test should have their employment cards stamped, higher rates of wages and transportation to and from work – like those employed in other public work schemes.[12] Their point of view was logical and may have stood up in a test case in court. The possibility existed however that the Northern Ireland courts may not have found in favour of Outdoor Relief workers, though an appeal to the House of Lords probably would have found in their favour.

Sam Kyle, moving the motion, pointed out that, according to the Government's own figures on the cost of living, Northern Ireland food as a whole cost 5 per cent more than elsewhere; some grocery stores appointed by the Guardians to supply food chits were taking a 25 per cent rake-off and that able-bodied unemployed were refused Outdoor Relief unless they applied for work to the Unemployment Exchange.[13] The most telling point in the debate came when Devlin quoted an influential Unionist, the Reverend T.M. Johnstone, speaking at a recent public meeting in Ballymoney, who said that the Government were following a 'leave-well-enough-alone' policy on the 25,000 at present on the list of employed.

> But there were 48,000 struck off the unemployed register during the previous twelve months... Many thousands of young people from 14–20 years who had never had a job... already many suicides owing to unemployment, local asylums crowded from the same causes. Poverty has increased during the year by 100 per cent, and the Board of Guardians have had to increase their meagre grants.[14]

Devlin challenged the Government to disprove what had been said in a public statement by one of their own leading supporters. The Minister of Labour promised to make a response to Devlin's points in his concluding remarks, but did not keep his promise. Neither did he comment on another and different case which Devlin raised. This concerned a family of six which the National Society for the Prevention of Cruelty to Children found living in Derry without fire, food or furniture. Mr Gordon, the local secretary of the NSPCC said that 'few of the dogs in the city would be in such a state of discomfort and starvation and that such cases were not uncommon'.

Opposition speakers accused the Government of falsifying figures of unemployment. They claimed that figures issued by the Minister of Labour related to those in receipt of unemployment benefit but did not include those who were unemployed and receiving no benefit or relief. The Minister admitted that he did not know the figure and had no record of them. The figure of 100,000 unemployed was mentioned by a number of Opposition speakers. It was never contradicted by front-bench spokesmen on the other side of the House, although the Government had claimed earlier that the figure was only half of that number.

On 30 January 1928 the Minister of Home Affairs wrote to the Guardians confirming his approval of the establishment of a labour test as a pre-condition to the granting of Outdoor Relief. It was blatant appeasement of the Guardians which was to have a boomerang effect on the Government over the next ten years.

An Order, made under Section 13, was issued by the Minister on 2 February 1928, with the additional condition that:

It shall be lawful under the Guardians to require any person receiving relief under the authority of this Order to perform such tasks of work as they may direct. The works on which the Guardians may employ the recipients of relief under the authority of this Order shall be such as may be approved by the Ministry.[15]

The first project under the new condition was the Whitewell housing expansion scheme which commenced on 27 February 1928. The land was owned by the Belfast Corporation and was to be developed as an additional housing estate. A further project was adopted to put drains in land on which an aerodrome was to be located in the Malone area of Belfast. Under the Order 37½ per cent of all money spent by Guardians on the projects would be refunded via the Belfast Corporation by the Government. The other 62½ per cent would come from the rates. The Whitewell project commenced on the first week in March under the briefest of arrangements and the barest of resources.

Tools had to be borrowed from the Belfast Corporation stores. Supervision and clerical assistance had to be recruited immediately on a temporary basis. It was decided, out of deference to the destitute workers' contribution to the scheme, to allow them to go to a second grocer in their area with their chits if they so desired. But nothing else had changed. Indeed, on 17 March a motion to pay half their relief in cash was defeated by seventeen votes to three.

Applicants for relief would be required to attend the local Dispensary where they would be issued with information on registration numbers, the number of days they were allowed to work, site location, tram tokens and the signature of the relieving officer. This information was to be brought to the supervisor of the work site. If no work was signed for by the site supervisor, then relief was stopped by the relieving officer. Work was to start each morning at 8.30 a.m. and would continue to 5 p.m., with one hour for lunch. All relief orders were issued on Saturday morning at times agreed with the relieving officers.

The Guardians went still further. They took the view, by introducing the labour test (thereby reducing the number of persons applying for and receiving special Outdoor Relief), that the need to apply for an Order under Section 13 no longer existed. A public statement was issued to that effect, which brought angry retorts from some members of the City Council who described the labour test scheme as 'inhuman slavery'. Certainly the Guardians were determined to use their powers against the able-bodied unemployed and appeared oblivious to the effects their exercise of power was having on the rest of the community. The Government, on the other hand, was not unmindful of the damage that could be done to the promotion of its strategy by the Guardians' growing indifference.

The Ministry of Home Affairs wrote to the Board to renew the Order, stating that they noted with concern the Guardians' intention not to apply for a further Order. The letter referred to the Guardians' own statistics to show that a number of genuine cases were still outside the labour test schemes and would be put to hardship if relief were stopped.[16] A further letter from the Ministry on 21 July expressed their great concern at the Guardians' decision not to apply for an Order. It pointed out that Parliament had placed a duty on them to relieve the poor. Failure to do so would place a very serious responsibility on them.[17]

The Guardians paid no heed to that letter which was followed by still another on 30 July from the Minister of Home Affairs himself. He wrote to say that he observed with the deepest regret that the Guardians had not altered their decision. He felt that they had not fully realised the serious situation and the great hardship to deserving persons which had been caused by that decision. The letter challenged the views of the Chairman, Mr John Wilson, JP, that it was not the committee's but the Government's duty to provide for able-bodied destitute persons. The Minister pointed out that only those persons who had paid weekly contributions to the Unemployment Insurance Fund were entitled to receive benefits from it: he said that the situation in itself was not a qualification for benefit. The Ministry administering the unemployment insurance scheme was no less bound to have regard to the conditions laid down by statute than were the Guardians to avail themselves of statutes designed to enable them to relieve destitution. It was clear, therefore, that the provision which had been made by the scheme did not in any way relieve the Guardians of their duties to the poor. The Government, by offering facilities to local authorities, had made an effort to increase the amount of work available so as to reduce the number of unemployed to the lowest possible figure; it in no way exempted the Guardians from their responsibility to relieve the able-bodied destitute.[18]

The Chairman of the Outdoor Relief Committee, who had by this time totally personalised the exchanges with the Ministry on this issue, drafted a reply which he brought to the meeting on 31 July 1928 for the Committee to adopt as their own. The Committee agreed to accept the draft which, according to the opposition on the Board, by now growing in volume, was a 'rehash of his own views'.

The Board met after the Outdoor Relief Committee. It resolved that the Ministry of Home Affairs be respectfully informed that, while the Board had decided not to renew their application for an Order under Section 13, it recognised that there might be cases where persons who, though not being able to procure a medical certificate, might suffer from physical and mental disabilities which would render their chances of getting employment practically nil in the present state of the labour market. Furthermore, the Board would be prepared to consider favourably such cases if the Ministry of Home Affairs would suggest measures to enable them to do so.

An informal conference was held sometime around the second week in August in the offices of the Ministry of Finance. The Ministers of Finance, Home Affairs and Labour were in attendance as well as their principal civil servants, representatives from the Belfast Corporation and the Board of Guardians. The meeting was confidential, rather like a Unionist Party meeting, because of the presence of the Ministry of Finance, Mr H.M. Pollock, acting as Prime Minister in the absence of Craig who was abroad on holiday.

Ostensibly, the idea behind the conference was for the Board to invite the Ministry of Home Affairs to suggest means whereby cases of need could be given adequate consideration. The Minister of Finance approved of an arrangement whereby the Guardians at their own discretion could relieve persons being the heads of families and unable to earn their living because of physical and mental incapacity.

It was clear from the Board of Guardians' minutes of 21 August 1928 that Pollock's role was much more than that of a benign Minister of Finance. He, with the other Ministers, had been brought back from annual holidays to put Wilson, in particular, and the Guardians in general, properly in their places. Consequently, Pollock, according to William A. Bell, one of the Board's delegation, pointed out the damage being done to the Party in the eyes of the public by the Guardians' refusal to carry out their statutory duty to the poor. He went on to threaten to replace them with Commissioners. R. Clements Lyttle denied this report of the meeting. It seemed to wash like a wave over the Chairman's head, who was also present at the meeting; that he had no comment to make about it speaks for itself! In any case the Ministry's next letter on the matter, received on 30 August, was welcomed by Wilson, and described as fair by him in the course of his very ample remarks from the chair. Major Brush represented the Ministry at this meeting and reported back to his Minister on the entirely different tone of the discussion.[19]

A new Order was made authorising the Guardians to grant relief outside the workhouse for a period of two months commencing 4 September 1928. It set out the new conditions as follows:

> Relief granted under the authority of this Order shall be given at the Guardians' discretion to such persons being the heads of families ordinarily resident in any of the said district electoral divisions who are able to satisfy the Guardians that they are physically or mentally in such a condition that they have not a reasonable chance of, and are handicapped in, obtaining employment, and who, for reasons satisfactory to the Guardians, are not in receipt of state benefit, and who are unable to obtain employment.

The Government was becoming increasingly apprehensive about the bad publicity the Party was receiving by the antics of the Guardians led by Wilson. He was seen by the public as representing a malign Unionism, particularly since the Guardians' public victory earlier in the year over the Government, when they forced upon them the concept of relief by labour test. Wilson and his colleagues had stated repeatedly in public 'that by their firmness in this regard they had saved the Belfast ratepayers thousands of pounds'.

The Government recognised that a constant display of arrogance by the Guardians towards the poor, which was becoming a feature of daily life in Belfast, could provoke the class struggle that they had been trying so diligently to avoid since they acquired power in 1920.

It was in the light of this reality that the Government decided to remove the granting of relief from the vagaries of Section 13 of the Local Government (Ireland) Act 1898 to the more solid foundation of a new Act – the Poor Relief (Exceptional Distress) Act (Northern Ireland) 1928. The Government calculated, on the basis of applying the new Act, that they and not the Guardians would be calling the tune.

The Opposition in Parliament, seeing the advantages of getting the

Bill through quickly, and in the process clipping the wings of the Guardians, expedited its passage through the various stages. By 30 October it had passed three stages before the Guardians made a move to discuss it.

Wilson, who had by that time vacated the chair in favour of Mrs Lily Coleman, opened with a tirade against the Government for introducing a Bill on Poor Relief without consulting the Belfast Board of Guardians. As usual, his speech to the committee was reported verbatim, purple patches and all, in the official minutes. He said, and his speech was printed in capital letters in the minutes, 'the Bill would pauperise and degrade working people of the Six Counties and would be administered with disastrous results to ratepayers'. He proposed that six objections should be stated and sent to the Minister as their considered views on the Bill.[20]

1. We protest strongly against the growth of legislation by regulation or conditions to be prescribed, undemocratic and unfair; and maintain that the principles under which Orders are contemplated, should be defined in the Bill.
2. The safeguard provided under Section 13 by the two public bodies elected by the electors and accountable to them is disregarded and no satisfactory plan made against extravagant expenditure such as brought ruin to certain districts in England.
3. That the description 'poor person, of any description' (not destitute poor person) would be an absolutely unwarranted, and, under certain conditions, a disastrous power to grant.
4. No period of residence is fixed as a condition precedent to giving such relief, thereby enabling a person just arrived from America or Cork to claim special relief.
5. That a Board of Guardians would have no reasonable grounds for refusing, under the Order when issued, to grant relief to applicants no matter how undesirable they might be.
6. Against the area of change fixed by the Bill. If a County Council felt that there was not sufficient reasons for the Order being issued in a District Electoral Division or Union, and refused to contribute, how could the ratepayers in the unfortunate District Electoral Division or Union area suffering from a period of distress pay the heavily increased burden.

Wilson's proposal, carried by 26 votes to 1, was duly sent to the Ministry of Home Affairs. The Ministry, conscious of past rebukes at the hands of the same Guardians, did not bother on this occasion to acknowledge the objections.

Debates on the Bill in Parliament were relatively civilised when compared with those of the Guardians and firmly focussed on whether or not the charge for relief of distress in Belfast should be a local or national charge. The Labour Opposition, joined by Devlin and Henderson, felt that the tendency in Britain was to make it a national charge and that they should follow suit here in using the legislative machinery thus created 'by forcing their arguments down the throats of the Belfast Board of Guardians.'[21]

Devlin's speech in support of Outdoor Relief payments being a charge on taxes, at the Committee stage of the debate on 23 October, was reported in the minutes. He said that:

> there were people who did not get unemployment allowance, people who were too proud to enter the workhouse or ask for Outdoor Relief, and poor people who were practically on the verge of starvation... and in the back lanes of our cities there are crowded dens of men and women who, through no fault of their own, are not insured and are suffering from starvation. It is only the least proud of them who go to the workhouse or ask for Outdoor Relief.

It emerged from these debates that Belfast had one-third of the population of Northern Ireland and one half of the unemployed – a fact which would lend support to the theory that the matter of relief was logically a national one – that it took nine shillings and three farthings to keep each person for a week in the workhouse against four shillings for an adult and two shillings for a child outside, over the same period.

Northern Ireland MPs were concentrating on the Poor Law issue at this time because they were aware that the Westminster Government had decided to abolish the entire concept of Poor Law; as an alternative they were working on a Parliamentary Bill to transfer its responsibilities to the more humane administrators of local government. The Northern Ireland Government was alerted to this development but appeared to have no desire to follow suit. Indeed the possibility existed that the Poor Relief (Exceptional Distress) Act (Northern Ireland) 1928, introduced several months before, may have been drafted to pre-empt pressure to abolish the Poor Law system in

Northern Ireland. The entire strategy for retaining power in Northern Ireland would have been at risk if the Government had lost control of the machinery for paying relief to the needy.

Throughout the Twenties long-term unemployment had forced more able-bodied men, skilled and unskilled, to look for relief than ever before. Poor Law Guardians had a crucial role in deciding who should receive relief and who should not. They knew what was required of them to make the strategy work – in spite of the over-zealous application of their powers.

To replace the Poor Law system, the new British system would have to be introduced. But that new system granted the right of every able-bodied person who was unemployed to relief by cash payments. The system was humane, and was what the poor, the trade unions and the Labour Party were agitating for throughout Britain.

The Unionist Government did not want that change, no matter how humane it might be. They wanted the Poor Law system to continue as it was because it enabled them to select those to whom they would give help. By employing discretion as to who should receive help they were in fact selecting whom they wanted to live in Northern Ireland. By abolishing that system and replacing it with the British system the principle of relief payments would have to change and everyone living in Northern Ireland would then secure relief as of right. If that were to happen their strategy was doomed. The Unionist Party knew that. They were too well ensconced in office and too well disciplined to have much trouble keeping the Labour MPs at bay on the issue.

In the course of one debate, Tom Henderson referred to the practice of publishing names of applicants for relief on local advertisement boards. The Minister of Home Affairs, replying, said that special relief cases were not advertised in public. Nevertheless, the Minister wrote on 17 November 1928 to the Guardians, referring to the change of duty under para. 12 of the Local Government Board 1904, which placed responsibility on relieving officers to make out a list of all people in receipt of Outdoor Relief and have it posted in public places as the Board of Guardians directed. The Minister proposed to have this duty removed from then on.

The Ministry indicated in a letter that it proposed to make an Order authorising the Board of Guardians to grant relief to able-bodied persons for three months subject to, firstly, relief being granted at Guardians' discretion to heads of families unable to obtain employment and not subject to other state benefit; secondly a full enquiry being held into family circumstances and thirdly, Indoor Relief being offered.[22]

The letter was not fully considered until the Board meeting of 8 January 1929. In the interim, however, it was known that a number of Guardians led by Wilson were on the verge of resigning because of what they believed was the Government's high-handed treatment of them 'in view of their long and noble service to the ratepayers'. In line with their logic, they recommended that regret be expressed over the Government's refusal to renew the Order under Section 13 which would deprive them of the power of granting Outdoor Relief to those suffering from disability. They did not refer to the Order made out by the Minister under the new Act. As far as they were concerned that Order had no relevance and they appeared not to have any intention of using it.[23]

The statement was typical of the arrogance of the Guardians. Once they realised that the Government was moving to reduce the mischief they were creating for the Party, they contrived to create more. The foregoing example was typical of this malignancy. The Government had given them more power in times of exceptional need and extended the period over which the Board could make grants. Nevertheless, the Board refused to use the Order, issuing a public statement instead, saying that the Government had stopped them from carrying out their statutory obligations to the poor. The Clerk of the Board, on the other hand, was beginning to see where his best interests lay. The new Act was designed to enable the Ministry of Home Affairs to take decisions affecting relief policies without regard to the discretion of the Guardians. Thus, off his own bat, the Clerk of the Board sent out directives to relieving officers to abide by the Government's Order.[24]

To save face the Guardians began to agitate for Government and Corporation members to meet them with a view to accelerating public work schemes which they felt would subject more relief recipients to labour tests. The Corporation members and the Government refused to meet them. The Guardians were extremely upset about 'having to authorise relief on the same scale as that being granted in England to able-bodied persons. The effects of these grants would be financially ruinous and disastrous, having regard to the valuation and heavy indebtedness cast on the city and rural districts comprising this Union.'[25]

The Minister of Home Affairs, Dawson Bates, was faced with a rogue elephant in the Belfast Guardians. He knew that if he could not have them guided back into line, his party would face an unnecessary loss of support, or worse, Westminster would step in to handle the matter of relieving destitution in Northern Ireland. By this time Westminster members were discussing the preliminary stages of a Bill to get rid of Poor Law Boards and have them replaced by a local government administration that would represent greater efficiency and fairness in its workings.

Bates had to have regard for this development and needed more than ever to hide the ugly nature of actions of the Belfast Guardians. He began to send his own lieutenants to attend Board meetings to keep the Guardians in line. These were military officers recruited by him as departmental inspectors when he set up his Ministry in 1921. It was commonly believed at the time that they would become his front-rank generals leading an army of 'B' Specials in the event of an attack on Northern Ireland's borders from Republicans in the Free State.

From 1927 onwards, when it became apparent that Wilson and his fellow Guardians were set on charging into a series of confrontations with the Government, Bates brought private pressure to bear on them from every direction to persuade them to keep their heads down while Boards of Guardians across the water were having theirs axed.

The Unionist Government needed the Belfast Guardians. They were an integral part of Unionist strategy to control votes for each election. They enabled 'last ditch' relief to be given to Unionist supporters who lost their eligibility to benefit from social security legislation. The Guardians were the instrument that enabled the Government to deprive the Catholic poor of relief by their powers of discretion. That discretion, in the hands of Unionist partisans, was a lot better for the Government than the alternative being proposed in the new legislation across the water – that all poor would have a right to cash benefit to meet their needs. That such a right extended to all citizens regardless of religion or party affiliation would be anathema to Unionist strategy.

To Bates, the proposal enshrined in the new Local Government Act passed at Westminster was unacceptable. Coupled with the higher birth rate of Catholics it would lead, he believed, to the Unionist Government being voted out of power. For all their excesses, the political danger involved in the continued existence of the Guardians was a risk worth taking as long as it meant that they would apply their powers selectively to deprive Catholics of relief while relieving the able-bodied unemployed who supported the Government.

110

Early in 1928, conferences were held between the Ministry, the Corporation and the Guardians on two occasions, 8 February and 12 March, to finalise the details of a scheme to get relief work. The following were agreed:

1. That allowances for special relief to able-bodied men employed under this work scheme shall in the first instance be paid by the Belfast Corporation and refunded directly to the Corporation by the Board of Guardians.

2. That the selection of men for this work be paid out of this fund and the decision as to the number of days they shall work rest with the Guardians.

3. That the amount of work shall be such that the weekly income would not exceed the equivalent of 75 per cent of a full week's wages: but reserving absolutely to the Guardians' discretion the amount to be allowed, and all cases to be dealt with on its merits, taking into account the entire circumstances of the investigation.

4. That the amount of special relief allowed be not less than the amount payable to a man working the number of days specified at the rate of wages usually paid on Unemployment Relief Schemes. Each man only to be paid for the time worked at this specific rate.

Both meetings were attended by two Ministry inspectors, Major Brush and Major Harris, who came as usual to supervise affairs. The Clerk was instructed to have a newspaper report criticising the Guardians sent to solicitors with a view to taking legal action against the newspaper involved. Two weeks later the Guardians were again complaining bitterly about a report in the *Northern Whig*, the leading Unionist newspaper, which referred to ill-treatment of two Protestant families by the Guardians. The Chairman said at the meeting that the reporter who wrote it had not the interest of the city at heart.

Four weeks later, on 12 March 1929, they complained of MPs being allowed to ask questions in Stormont regarding decisions which they had taken in relieving individual cases of distress. They challenged the right of the Minister of Home Affairs to receive and disseminate detailed information on such cases. Beattie, angry at this arrogance, promptly asked the Speaker to rule on what was an MP's right in such matters and was assured by the Speaker that the Guardians were technically in breach of privilege. However, the matter was left to rest at this point. It was feared that to pursue it beyond that would create the opportunity for certain Guardians to come to the House to defend their policy in the full glare of publicity.[26] Even Labour MPs baulked at that prospect!

A certain amount of support did exist for the Guardians among other members of the petit bourgeoisie who dominated the middle level of the Glengall Street machine. The Guardians were seen as the only body pushing back the tide of unlimited charity to working-class malingerers. Certain members of the Protestant churches, not too well-disposed to the Catholic attitude on birth control, could always be relied upon to resist any measure of social assistance being extended to this deprived section of the community. Such was the case when a delegation of four clergymen, led by an ex-military captain, arrived early in March at the Board to congratulate them on their stand against this 'wastrel class' and to urge them 'to cut off grants to parasites'.[26]

The Order issued by the Ministry on 19 December 1928 was revoked and a new one sent to the Guardians similar in content but with additions based on what had been agreed between the representatives of the three bodies at the Conference on 12 March.

Work on the first scheme of street resurfacing – public works – commenced on 11 April 1929. Sixteen men were employed. They had each been given a card by their relieving officers on which was written the work to be done, the time and the place. The foreman, on receiving it, perforated it and returned it with a chit for groceries to correspond with the amount of work done. The amounts granted and the work done was posted up in the relieving officer's office for the public to see.

Men working on the relief scheme were to be insured in case of an accident under the National Insurance Act, but not under the Unemployment Insurance Act. That meant that if they had an accident they could apply for sickness benefit but were not entitled to unemployment benefit. The Minister of Labour had given a ruling earlier that the persons concerned were not working a full week and therefore could not be deemed to be employed persons within the meaning of the Act. By 30 September 1929, 325 able-bodied men had been given work under the scheme and had been paid a total figure of £2,370 4s.7d.[27] It was clear that unemployment insurance stamps should have been paid by the Guardians as employing agents. The Government had only to amend the Act as they had done with other social security legislation, but that would have meant changing the status of the relief workers and giving them the right to receive unemployment benefit.

Allegations continued to be made throughout this period by MPs about the selection of certain workers on a religious basis in the scheme. Nationalist MPs were most vociferous on this issue. Labour MPs drew attention to their own quota of cases. The Belfast Harbour Commission had an arrangement with relieving officers to send only the 'appropriate type' of workers with a letter of recommendation to them. The most notable case, however, was raised at Stormont on 6 October 1931, by way of a parliamentary question. It gave information of a road construction project that was operating under the green card system which involved Catholic workers but which was suddenly changed to provide contract work. The 'green card' men were dismissed to allow for the introduction of private contract work which enabled Government supporters from the Minister of Labour's own constituency to complete the job.[28]

A newly-elected MP, Mr J.W. Nixon, complained to the Minister of Home Affairs on 10 April 1930, that some relieving officers required recipients of Outdoor Relief to assemble at points along main roads at considerable distances from their homes. Some of the recipients who were very sick, old and on crutches, were required to remain for hours in rain before relieving officers arrived to give them their chits.[29]

In Parliament other events were happening that were to have far-reaching effects on the Labour Opposition and on the future of Northern Ireland. The diminishing Unionist majority, which had fallen from forty to thirty-three after the general election in 1925, had caused considerable alarm in the Unionist camp. The Government had decided, in view of the results, to abolish proportional representation for a single, non-transferable voting system. In preparation for the election in 1929, the Unionists moved an amendment to abolish the PR system under the Government of Ireland Act 1920. It was carried by a large majority.[30]

McMullen and Kyle, the most effective of the Labour men, were defeated at the polls under the new voting system which the Unionist Government predicted would reduce political alignments to those of the two religious tribes.

Devlin supported a slum landlord and publican against McMullen in the election and this contributed largely to his defeat. Though he won himself, Devlin gradually abandoned parliamentary procedure, turning up infrequently at Stormont until his death in 1934.

Meanwhile, agitation against the Poor Law Guardians was increasing rapidly. It was known that the Poor Law had been abolished across the water the previous year and that the reasons for its abolition were equally applicable to Northern Ireland. The Unemployed Workers' Committee, which had a connection with other workers' committees in the major cities of Britain, began to receive more support in Belfast for their efforts to get rid of the hated Guardians.

Another organisation, calling itself the Outdoor Relief Workers, was founded. Its aim was to improve the lot of the Outdoor Relief workers by taking the place of the trade union representation of which they had been deprived as a condition of employment.

The number of cases seeking relief had risen sharply from 24 per month in 1930 to 238 per month in 1931. In the past increased numbers of cases invariably led to a reduction in the amount granted on the grocery chits. Such was the Guardians' practice. The Chairman of the Board, commenting on the situation on 5 May 1931, said that they were required to take serious notice of the increased expenditure on Outdoor Relief. They existed only as a Board to relieve the destitute and infirm. Harry Diamond, a Guardian representing a Catholic area, replied that the Board was too stringent in its dealings with the poor, and cited the example of the St Vincent de Paul Society which had given out cash grants of £700 to meet high rents in the Whiterock area of West Belfast.[31]

The Outdoor Relief Committee had met the day before and recommended to the Board, who endorsed the recommendation, that all cases of Outdoor Relief after twelve months be discontinued and that in future all cases in receipt of relief for six months' continuous payment be brought to the notice of the Outdoor Relief Committee by relieving officers.[32]

On 19 May a letter was received by the Board asking that it consider receiving a delegation from the Central Committee of Outdoor Relief Workers who wished to discuss three points:

1. That no man be forced into the workhouse. If no work is available then he should receive relief.

2. That relief granted should be equal to the rate paid out in money at the Unemployment Exchange.

3. That unemployment insurance stamps should be affixed to insurance cards on the first day of each week.[33]

The delegation was kept waiting outside the locked gates of the workhouse, and by a vote of the Guardians of 20 to 3 they were refused entrance. A letter from the Trades Council, which was received on the same day concerning the issue of increased relief rates, was marked 'read' by an unanimous decision of the Board.[34]

Both workers' organisations were entirely dissatisfied with the replies that they had received from the Board and re-submitted requests for delegations to be heard on 26 May 1931, and again on 2 June. They were turned down on each occasion by overwhelming votes of the Board. Newspapers covering the 2 June meeting reported that hostile comments were made on the impertinence of workers seeking a meeting with the Board. They were described as representing 'Bolshevism of the worst type' by the new chairman, Mr A. McKegney, JP.

The relationship between the Belfast Guardians and the Government had deteriorated over the years since 1921. Starting from the point at which total agreement was secured on common strategy, they seemed afterwards to develop in separate directions. The Government set up institutions in its own mould by ruthlessly exorcising Catholics from positions of responsibility in the early Twenties and Labour politicians from Parliamentary life in the late Twenties by abolishing PR. By so doing they seemed to have found the perfect plan for a permanent hegemony in Northern Ireland. It seemed now to be falling apart because of the Guardians' inability to handle the powers bestowed on them to make the Party strategy work.

As the last few years had proven, the Guardians had become intoxicated with their own importance in the Unionist plan. As Craig, Bates and Andrews acquired populist tendencies as well as increased resources to compensate their working-class supporters for hurt feelings, the Government got the popularity; the Poor Law Guardians got the odium. A collision of interests that was to put the whole strategy under unprecedented strain was imminent.

8
Outdoor Relief Riots 1932

Unemployment in Belfast, bad enough in the Twenties, worsened at the beginning of the Thirties, and with it the frustration of the unemployed workers with Unionist politicians.

That part of their strategy to keep Protestant workers in employment while excluding Catholics came adrift as the volume of jobs throughout Northern Ireland diminished. The second part of their strategy which should have been operating to provide relief to the unemployed Protestants had broken down as well, because the Government's hostile attitude to the Poor Law Guardians caused them in retaliation to deny relief to Catholic and Protestant alike. This development was not part of the strategy. Indeed it was likely to defeat the strategy in that it created a new class unity of unemployed workers to confront the Government on economic matters.

This was the one development that the Unionist Government and the Belfast bourgeoisie had always feared. In England and in other European countries when Labour politicians secured enough popular support they were elected to Government. It followed, therefore, that the development of Labour or class politics would bring the same results in Northern Ireland. However, with the community divided on a religious basis, Labour could have no hope of getting into government to legislate for reforms to favour its own class. Neither, for that matter, could the Catholic politicians, for they too were confined by their own limited political platform to a permanent minority role.

This position which the Unionist Government wished to maintain was now in jeopardy because of the alienation of the Guardians from the Government and its strategy. The Guardians for their part felt bitter about the Government's failure to acknowledge the fine work they had done in the past in keeping the rates down and in forcing malingerers to work. In retaliation for the Government's indifference to their special 'skills', the Guardians continued to cut and refuse relief

116

to the mounting number of destitute.

The situation became desperate in 1932. Half the 100,000 unemployed of Northern Ireland lived in Belfast: 42,710 received statutory benefit; 19,380 received transitional benefit; 13,908 received no benefit; the rest, made up of single able-bodied youths, were not registered for employment and were excluded from relief rolls. There was little hope of immediate improvement because Belfast's traditional industries, ship-building and linen, were in the grip of a deep recession.

Due to the long-term nature of this unemployment many of the able-bodied were forced to seek relief through the Poor Law system when their unemployment insurance benefits had run out. Many of these workers, regarded as having worked in insurable employment, were still enjoying transitional benefit which they received at the discretion of the Guardians – a concept which the Government sought to build into their social legislation. These were the special arrangements that the Government made to cater for its supporters. By 1932 the number of long-term unemployed was multiplying; people were being forced out of the unemployment insurance cycle and being missed by the Outdoor Relief net which normally would catch them for relief payments. In normal times the system which the Unionists built could protect their own supporters but in these circumstances, in which too little money was left from the rates, it could not. The year 1932 was abnormal in that there was too little work, too little goodwill in the relationship between the Government and the Guardians, too little charity in the hearts of the Guardians for the unemployed and too little bread for the hungry. It was a high grade recipe for social upheaval and that was exactly what it created.

The social upheaval was not confined to Belfast; other cities like Glasgow, Bristol, Birmingham, Newcastle and London were experiencing similar conditions. From early in the year people, incensed at the increased unemployment figures, the reduction of unemployment benefits and the hated means test, were taking to the main roads of British cities to show their opposition to Government policies.

Demonstrations and Hunger Marches were organised throughout Britain by the National Unemployed Workers Movement. It was part of a large-scale campaign, initiated at a conference held in Shoreditch Town Hall and attended by 657 delegates from areas in England, Scotland and Wales.

The campaign was to be built around the signing of a monster petition containing four demands:

1. the abolition of the means test;
2. the abolition of the Anomalies Act;
3. the restoration of the 10 per cent Unemployment Benefits cuts;
4. the restoration of the cuts that had been made in the social services.

The campaign was strongly supported. Clashes with the police were daily occurrences and many of the local leaders were arrested. The worst clash occurred in Birkenhead on 13 September when a crowd of 10,000 protesters were baton-charged by a large force of police. The clash was unnecessary as the protesters' demands had been met by the recently-constituted Public Assistance Board. The police charged as the crowd were good-humouredly receiving information of their demands having been met. One hundred protesters were taken to hospital where one died of his injuries. Forty-five others were arrested and charged in the courts, some of the leaders receiving two years' imprisonment.

The police behaviour immediately provoked larger demonstrations in the area. Liverpool followed and other shipbuilding areas like South Shields, Newcastle and Glasgow organised demonstrations that were as much against police behaviour as against the reforms of the Public Assistance Committee.

In Britain the category of able-bodied unemployed was catered for under legislation introduced in 1929 which transferred responsibility for relief to local authority units. In Northern Ireland the same legislation did not apply. Here, a Public Assistance Committee was established under the control of the Poor Law Guardians to examine the merits of individual applications from able-bodied unemployed. But little change flowed from the deliberations of the Committee, as distinct from Britain where substantial change for the better resulted.

The Belfast Board of Guardians gave grants only to applicants who qualified under the 1929 Act. In spite of this attitude the number of persons in receipt of exceptional distress relief in Belfast sharply increased as is clear by the comparison set out in the following table:

Date	No. of cases	No. of persons	Amount paid in wages	Amount paid in kind
31 Jan. 1931	292	137	£191. 1. 1.	£ 60. 14. 0.
6 Feb. 1932	1,038	4,767	£368.19. 1.	£459. 19. 0.

By 1932 some of those on relief work were being paid in cash and others in kind.[2]

At the beginning of 1932 the Belfast City Councillors, apprehensive of the effects that an increase of rates might have on ratepayers, sought a conference with the Poor Law Guardians with the object of reducing the number of applicants. The Guardians met them on 16 February and, mindful of their statutory obligations, agreed to a joint approach being made to the Ministry of Home Affairs with a view to securing increased grants towards the costs of unemployment relief and distress relief schemes.

Pollock, the Minister of Home Affairs, replied on 13 April saying that, though he wanted the schemes to develop, he was facing considerable difficulties in getting further grants for them from the Road Fund. (The Government grant to the Belfast Corporation was 25 per cent of the total cost.[3]) He was referring to a disagreement between himself on the one hand and the Prime Minister and the anti-populist group on the other over the matter of expanding relief schemes to meet the increasing number of unemployed. The British Treasury had intervened on several occasions that year to prevent further use of public work schemes as an aid to economic recovery. Pollock was obviously determined to impose that directive on Northern Ireland. Bates thought that he had more urgent and compelling reasons for disregarding the directive. He submitted a memorandum to the Cabinet on his reasons:

> All my information shows that unless adequate measures are taken in good time, there is grave danger that the peace of the province will be endangered... the only alternative to relief measures is to keep order by force and for this purpose, in the face of widespread discontent, the existing force is not adequate... it will be necessary to have relief works on a large scale in the coming months and ·it will be necessary for the Government to assist by way of grants.[4]

Bates had been raiding the Road Fund for several years prior to this to underwrite the cost of relief schemes and was likely to continue in view of what he had said in his memo to the Cabinet.

Pollock became alarmed that the continued expenditure on relief schemes would get the Government into serious trouble with Westminster. Accordingly, he wrote to Craig on 3 October, seeking assurances that no burden would be placed on the budget without his full knowledge. Craig readily agreed. However, the following month, with Craig's full support, Bates arranged for the payment of £200,000 from the Road Fund to meet the liabilities incurred in relief schemes.

Spender wrote of this in his diary, 28 November 1932.

> The true facts have now come to light, namely, that the Minister of Home Affairs has approved of very heavy grants being made to local authorities from the Road Fund which is under his control and that, having authorised such contributions from the Government, he now says they have to be met from the Exchequer although the Minister of Finance has never been consulted about the matter. I cannot imagine any other country where such a state of affairs could be possible.

Spender and Pollock campaigned vigorously to resist increased expenditure because of the fear that their annual budget would not balance. They feared that expenditure for social services and relief purposes would destroy the efforts industrialists were making to make the economy healthy. The matter had been sharpened at a Cabinet meeting on 23 January 1931 when Andrews spoke strongly on what could be done by the Government to create more jobs. Several days later, after consultation with his Minister, Spender wrote to Craig stating that too much was being done for the working classes. He cited in his letter that wholesale prices were below pre-war level, retail prices had been falling over the previous six years and that fewer hours were being worked without a corresponding reduction of pay, while workers were receiving other benefits from taxation, insurance, pensions, education and housing grants.

Earlier in the year Bates had announced the Government's decision to increase the grant for distress relief works to 50 per cent. The City Council was contacted several times throughout the summer by the Guardians with information on the rising number of relief recipients: the number had risen to 1,200 while only one-third of that number was engaged on work schemes.

A special meeting of the Board of Guardians was held on 21 June to review the whole question of relief to the able-bodied. By this time the payment for relief had amounted to £1,546 per week, of which £1,131 was in 'kind' and £415 in wages: 488 men were engaged on relief schemes and another 1,300 were available for work. Had these men been engaged in work another £565 per week and 2,600 days' work would have been forthcoming under the new arrangements with the Government. The extra numbers applying for relief added two extra days of committee work for Board members; this extension was needed to process the applications which tended to come almost entirely from the young and single members of the community.[5]

In the Northern Ireland Parliament constant references were being made to the growing crises affecting the poor in Belfast. The most significant of these were made by Jack Beattie, the sole Labour MP in the House, and Joseph Devlin, who had returned once more for the debate on the Outdoor Relief crisis.

Beattie complained that the Government was using the new Public Assistance Board in a party-political way. He said that the Board was working along the same lines as were the Poor Law Guardians. 'You have your inspectors, you have your Board of Guardians, the same basis of calculation, the same mentality as associated with Outdoor Relief – all doing the same job for you.'[6]

Devlin, speaking in the debate, referred to the Belfast Board of Guardians as the worst in Europe, 'a body without respect for the dignity of labour... people were at their wits' end trying to hold on to a home with not one penny left for clothing, boots and replenishments'. He claimed further that relief across the water was greater than that paid by the Public Assistance Board in Belfast.[7]

The *Belfast News-Letter*, a leading Unionist daily paper, published figures on 4 October 1932 which confirmed Devlin's charges. In Manchester a man with a wife and one child received 21s. per week; in Liverpool a similar family received 23s; in Glasgow, 25s. 3d.; in Bradford, 26s.; in Northampton, 27s.; and in some cases extra allowances were granted for rent. In Belfast the normal Outdoor Relief grant for the same size of family was 12s. If work was available the head of the household would be given 1½ to 2½ days' work. The payment would be in cash. If no work was available it would be in kind.

Earlier that year Devlin, supported this time by Henderson, launched an attack on the Minister of Home Affairs for appointing Vice-Admiral Archdale, a brother of the Minister of Agriculture, to his staff with special responsibility for the Belfast Guardians. Archdale was retired on a pension from the Navy, had wide land-owning interests and was regarded as a senior figure in Unionist and Orange circles. His appointment was viewed by the Opposition as an additional instrument for keeping the Guardians in line. Indeed, the Opposition's view of his role was correct, because he was reported later in the Poor Law Minutes as removing physically from the East Belfast office a Unionist Guardian who was persistently intervening with staff on applicants' behalf. Devlin attacked Archdale again for advising Boards to refuse Outdoor Relief to those destitutes not favourably disposed to the Government.

By late summer the storm clouds were gathering. Jack Beattie, inspired by a large measure of public support, hit the Ulster Parliament on 30 September like a whirlwind. It was the first day after the summer holidays and the first Parliamentary session to be held at Stormont. There had been no meeting for four months and it was decided to adjourn after a two-hour sitting for another two months. Anticipating that the Government would want to avoid discussion of the approaching storm over relief of to the unemployed, Beattie put down a motion on the Order Paper concerning the seriousness of the unemployment situation. He believed that a motion set out under this heading, provided the form and terms were right, would enable him to get the entire Outdoor Relief problem debated.[8] The Speaker ruled his motion out of order because it was controversial. He accepted an innocuous motion from the Government which thanked the Lord Mayor, Town Clerk and Councillors of Belfast for their courtesy during the time the Government had use of the Belfast City Hall while the Parliament building at Stormont was under construction.

Seeing through the Government's ploy to abort the debate, Beattie lifted the mace and threw it under the table which held the despatch box. The Sergeant-at-Arms, with a certain aount of pomp, replaced it in its cradle, but Beattie, getting madder by the minute, grabbed it again and advanced towards the Speaker. Before being overcome by sheer weight of numbers he attempted to throw the mace at the Speaker. It fell short unfortunately. The police were called and Beattie was ordered from the House.

The Government tactic in avoiding a debate and the treatment of Jack Beattie gained the Outdoor Relief workers new support and set the temper for immediate exchanges on the issue.

On 2 October the *Belfast News-Letter* said in its editorial:

The problem of distressed unemployed is forcing itself or being forced upon the attention of the community generally. Winter approaches, the church clergy, heads of church missions, lay social workers and others state that at no time within their experience were there such poverty and need as exist at present. We are told that those on Outdoor Relief are on the verge of starvation; unless something is done and done quickly, conditions will become tragically worse... Wholesale admissions to the workhouse – if that be an alternative – offers no scope for economy. The burden of taxation is well-nigh intolerable and yet if a reasonably increased levy for the purpose of the Board of Guardians would help to tide us over the winter we hesitate to believe that the rate-payers, as a body, would be found protesting.

Two days later the *News-Letter* reported that the United Unionist Labour Association had passed a resolution which stated that they felt it absolutely necessary that the amount given in Outdoor Relief should be considerably increased. Craig and Bates both realised the significance of the UULA statement. They knew that the basis of their power lay in helping the skilled workers and this resolution showed that the skilled workers' support of the Northern Ireland Government was wavering because the Poor Law Guardians, by their public parsimony, were alienating them.

By late August the Dispensaries were inundated with new applicants and the relieving officers were unable to cope with the work. The relieving officers reported to the Board that in the week ending 20 August 1932 there were 2,480 recipients of relief in counties Down and Antrim as opposed to 550 recipients in the corresponding week of 1931.[9] The figures left the Guardians in a state of shock. As a result they were forced to appoint nine extra assistants to help the nine relieving officers with the backlog of cases, some of them held back for eight weeks, as well as the reassessment of current cases which they had not the manpower to cope with.

James Collins, an Irish Nationalist always in conflict with the Guardians, gave notice of a motion which demanded that from 1 October a supplementary grant of 10s. in cash be awarded to all recipients of Outdoor Relief. On 20 September Collins moved his motion stating that the current scale of relief compared very unfavourably with that made to the same categories of needy in Britain.

The Chairman in reply said that they should turn down the motion because the mover always held the other members up to contempt and ridicule and that each person should see that his family was 'regulated'. Another Unionist said that it was unfair to bring children into the world without provision being made to maintain them.[10] The motion was lost by twenty votes to two.

This form of escapism was no proof against the explosion that was building up outside the workhouse gates. Through the month of September street demonstrations were getting bigger, becoming more frequent and angry in mood as support for the unemployed grew. The Trades Council and the two general workers' unions, the Amalgamated Transport & General Workers' Union (ATGWU) and the Irish Transport & General Workers' Union (ITGWU), kept pressure on the Guardians to meet them to discuss the low rates paid to the employed. The craft unions once more were not to the fore, apart from those members who attended as delegates to the Trades Council or were individually angered by the Guardians' treatment of the unemployed.

The Rev. John N. Spence, superintendent of the Belfast Central Mission, asked for permission to bring a delegation representing businessmen and clergymen to encourage the Guardians to increase the scale of grants. He had earlier written to the newspapers to say that in seventeen large British cities chosen at random, the average rate of wages per head was £4 3.0. and in Belfast less than £2 10.0. per head was paid, while the food consumption rate was greatly lower. The delegation arrived at the next meeting and before being allowed to address the Board, was lectured by the Chairman on the intrinsic goodness of the 'work ethic' which, he assured the delegation, was fundamental to Northern Ireland society. The point of the sermon seemed to be that jobs were available but that the destitute of Belfast would not take them up. The Guardians could not be convinced that there was no work in Belfast.

The minutes of this meeting show that a relieving officer was reprimanded for giving out food dockets on a temporary basis to the extent of £2 8.0. which were not finally authorised. His responsibility covered this contingency but was subject to authorisation by the Guardians at their next meeting. The relieving officer was made to pay the sum back out of his own pocket.[11]

Meanwhile, other factors were developing that were to give the crisis unexpected shape. The unemployed workers' agitation, which had been on the increase since 1931, began to take a sharper edge.

A small group of revolutionary workers in the Unemployed Workers' Movement, who were delegates to the Belfast Trades Council, set up an organisation to agitate for improvement in the wages and working conditions of the Outdoor Relief workers and, more generally, to assist the destitute.[12]

Tommy Geehan, one of the delegates to the Trades Council, called for and received support for a strike amongst Outdoor Relief workers. A mass meeting held on 30 September and attended by 2,000 relief workers was convened as a result of his call and a decision was taken to strike unless the following demands were met:

1. Abolition of task work (i.e. labour test to qualify for relief).
2. Increase in scale of relief to a man of 15s. 3d. per week, wife 8s. 3d. per week, each child 2s.
3. No payment in kind – all relief to be paid in cash.
4. Street improvement work under Exceptional Distress Relief Scheme, or scheme of like character, to be done at trade union rate of wages.
5. Adequate outdoor allowance to all single men and women who are unemployed and not in receipt of unemployment benefit.[13]

This was the first occasion since 1919 on which the Belfast proletariat had organised into a single unit to oppose the bourgeoisie on a class issue. It was the moment for which the Revolutionary Workers Group, led by Tommy Geehan and Betty Sinclair, had been waiting. They realised the potential in this grim situation for the creation of class politics – to get rid of the Unionist stranglehold on the body politic and defeat the bourgeois strategy for controlling the apparatus of government. A date for a strike was set for 4 October. Preparations were made by local district committees to co-ordinate food provision activities and provide support for relief workers.

On Monday, 3 October, 600 Outdoor Relief men who were due to start work that day went on strike in support of their demands for increased allowances. The pickets which were mounted at all sites led to their closure. The strike was completely effective.

That evening, with their supporters, numbering around 60,000 of both religions, they marched from the Labour Exchange in Frederick Street to the traditional 'free-speech' forum at the Custom House steps where four platforms of speakers addressed the vast crowds. It was a torch-light parade, led by bands which, to avoid giving religious offence, played the neutral tune, 'Yes, We have no Bananas' over and over again.[14]

The main speakers at the meeting were Jack Beattie, MP, the two sympathetic Poor Law Guardians, Harry Diamond and James Collins, as well as Tommy Geehan and Betty Sinclair of the Belfast Trades Council. The meeting renewed its demand for increased rates of relief and added a call for a rent and 'tick' (hire purchase payment) strike.[15]

On the following day 7,000 unemployed marched to the workhouse on the Lisburn Road where the Guardians usually met. Thousands lay on the road, one of Belfast's main arteries, blocking all traffic. A deputation was received this time by the Guardians and reiterated their demand for a minimum of 15s. 3d. for a single man and 13s. 6d. for a single woman each week, all payments to be made in cash, and the end of the means test and task work. The Chairman, Mr J. Wilson, had been informed by Collins before the delegation arrived that if he influenced the Board not to receive the delegation he would live to regret it.[16]

There was little doubt as to the validity of that advice because the crowd which had swollen enormously during the course of the demonstration were heartily singing parodies of their favourite songs with words appropriate to the occasion. They remained there for three hours before marching to their homes using the main thoroughfares of Belfast. Shop windows were broken on the way.

The Board's response was to pass a resolution which was passed on to the Government, pointing out that the responsibility which they had was already too great, and that they felt it was up to the Government to see that other arrangements were made to provide for unemployed single persons.[17]

On Wednesday 5 October, the police prevented another march to the workhouse by lining the route with Crossley tenders and Lancia armoured cars. Nevertheless, demonstrators infiltrated the police lines and 144 were admitted to the workhouse as inmates. Once inside they refused to take orders and were reported singing and dancing throughout the night. Three were arrested and removed from the workhouse premises. Two were subsequently released after giving an undertaking on future behaviour. The other was sent to prison for a month for disorderly behaviour.

By nightfall, crowds were spilling over into the main roads of Belfast and serious rioting broke out in several places. A tram was hijacked, more shop windows broken and shops looted in the main Catholic and Protestant ghetto areas. Batons were drawn and crowds constantly charged wherever they were visible to the police. For the rest of the week the rioting continued unabated.

On Monday, 10 October, the Lord Mayor of Belfast, Sir Crawford McCullagh, requested an immediate conference with the Chairman of the Belfast Board of Guardians. He had been visited the night before by an authoritative group of Belfast's leading businessmen and officials from the craft unions who expressed fears concerning the implications of the rioting and asked for the Lord Mayor's intervention.

The meeting, held in the Lord Mayor's Parlour in the City Hall, was attended as usual by Vice-Admiral Archdale, the Lord Mayor and Board representatives including the Chairman of the Board. It was announced after the meeting that a new range of relief schemes would immediately be organised which would be paid to all men on relief and, with the increased work available, give increases of payment for extra time worked. Moreover, it was proposed by the Government to increase the grants for relief schemes by 50 per cent.[18]

An Extraordinary Meeting of the Guardians was convened for that afternoon to hear a report on the conference with the Lord Mayor. The report was given and the Chairman congratulated, according to the minutes, on his fine work in finding a solution. He accepted the praise without demur.[19] Collins, predicting that the increase was not adequate in scale or in scope, moved an amendment to the report for the British scales to apply to all cases of relief at once. He was, as usual, ruled out of order by the Chairman.[20]

As anticipated by Collins, the strikers, at a meeting in St Mary's Hall, turned down the Board's offer on the grounds that it was not adequate. They wanted full trade union rates for all work done, an increased rate on the Outdoor Relief schemes and a general strike of all workers in the city to support them.

The Outdoor Relief workers, to escalate the campaign, commenced to organise meetings in the coming week and planned a monster demonstration for Tuesday, 11 October, which would include marches from every district to a meeting point in the centre of Belfast. It was proposed to march to the Custom House steps for a mass rally in support of the Outdoor Relief workers.

The Belfast Strike Committee had established a food depot in York Street by Monday, 10 October. The ITGWU ran one in Corporation Street which served the Docks area with signal success. Sympathisers donated £300. Dockers and carters toured the large firms in the Docks area daily and collected 4,927 loaves, 800 stones of potatoes, 727 lbs.

of sugar, 170 lbs. of tea, 91 lbs. of butter, 131 pots of jam, 16 stone of flour. The Belfast Co-Operative Society gave 500 gallons of milk and another firm 1,000 packets of oatmeal. The dockers made these up in parcels and gave them out with money grants to local unemployed and their dependents. (One helper, sent to a bank with a five-pound note to get half-crowns, absconded with the money. He was seen on the Liverpool boat that night but never returned to Belfast.[21])

News broke early the following morning that the Parliamentary Secretary to the Ministry of Home Affairs, G.B. Hanna, MP, on behalf of the Government, had banned all public meetings for that day and the day following under the Special Powers Act; and that he was drafting into Belfast another 700 police from outlying areas and asking for the military in Holywood to be given stand-by duties.[22]

Letters sent by Sir Charles Wickham, Inspector-General of the Royal Ulster Constabulary, to the Minister of Home Affairs, and his reports at Cabinet meetings for 1932, state in unequivocal terms that the police were not confident that they had the capacity to cope with the difficulties that would emanate from large-scale rioting. Earlier in the year the police had experienced such a situation when heavy rioting had broken out during the Eucharistic Congress. They had been barely able to cope with those events. They were saved only because the Inspector-General had scoured the countryside in a successful attempt to bring additional men to Belfast. Bates raised the matter at the August Cabinet meeting and was given approval to recruit sixty more men to raise the police numbers to full strength, and further approval to bring back the 'B' Specials for two drills a week.[23] With this information in mind, Bates, with Craig's and Andrews' help, became the prime mover in ultimately forcing the Cabinet to find the extra money for Outdoor Relief purposes.

Tommy Geehan spoke to a gathering of strikers' wives in St Mary's Hall on 10 October. He was reported in the press as saying:

For many years the workers in Belfast have been divided by artificial barriers of religion and politics, but the past two months has witnessed a wonderful spectacle, because the workers were never united on a common platform, demanding the right to live. Tomorrow you will see the mightiest demonstration of unity that has ever been seen in Belfast. The authorities have banned the demonstration tomorrow but the workers are going out.[24]

On Tuesday, 11 October, the unemployed attempted to resist the ban and riots spread like wildfire throughout the city. They were intensive in the working-class areas of East, West and North Belfast, especially at the specified starting points of the march. Cobble stones and 'kidney-pavers' (round stones which could be thrown with effect) were collected, picks and shovels were retrieved from work depots and barricades erected. In some places trenches were dug to hamper the movement of police vehicles. Someone had attempted to plan and co-ordinate tactics againt the police.[25] The subsequent activity was coherent and effective.

The scene was described by James Kelly, a journalist with the *Irish Independent*:

> When Orangemen and Catholics, the lines of starvation already etched on their hollow cheeks gripped hands and declared emotionally 'Never again will they divide us' there was consternation in the ranks of professional politicians... On the Shankill Road crowds of growling men lounged around waiting... Suddenly a big red-faced woman with a black shawl thrown over her shoulders, wisps of hair hanging from her eyes, appeared almost from nowhere... She ran to crowds of men and in quick, terse language told them that the unemployed and the police were in conflict on the Falls Road. 'Are you going to let them down?' she almost shrieked. 'No, by heavens we are not', they roared back, and in almost a twinkling a veritable orgy of destruction began.[26]

The police moved towards these areas in large numbers heavily armed and backed up with armoured cars in an attempt to take over the main roads of Belfast. They were attacked by stone throwers once they moved towards the side streets and were driven back on to the main roads. On the Falls Road the mill workers, many of them in their bare feet, broke up the police cordons, reportedly to allow food supplies into the beleagured north and west areas of Belfast. By late afternoon the police had opened fire and proclaimed a curfew from 11 p.m. until 5 a.m. the following morning.

The next day barricades were still up and hijackings were taking place frequently throughout the city. By that afternoon the Government's tactics were becoming clear – they were now shooting with effect in the Catholic areas of the Falls Road while baton-charging in others.

Police again stopped food supplies coming into Belfast and rounded up hundreds of men in Catholic areas to dismantle the barricades. James Collins, a member of the Board of Guardians and a City Councillor, was dragged out of his house with his son at gun-point and made to take down barricades close to his home in the Short Strand. He was only partly dressed but was forced to work all night in the rain under threat of being shot. By this time, two strike leaders were in jail and over a hundred others arrested on rioting charges.[27]

John Campbell, a Guardian and secretary of the Labour Party, commenting on the rioting stated that 'Lord Craigavon's solution was to divide the workers into different religious camps and it was noteworthy that although the recent trouble was spread all over the city only in a Roman Catholic area did the police use their guns'.

Campbell was quite right. Bates had issued instructions to the police, not merely to contain the rioting, but to use firearms in Catholic areas purportedly to prevent the IRA from overthrowing the Government, and to use batons in Protestant areas purportedly to stop looting of shops by troublemakers. By employing these tactics the Unionist Government could conceal from England and other countries the real reasons for the rioting and at the same time contrive to keep both sides of the community separated by the threat of the IRA using the Outdoor Relief strike to attack the state.

When the rioting stopped, two people had been shot dead. Another fifteen had suffered gunshot wounds – all in Catholic areas and inflicted by the police. Nineteen others suffered injuries. The following was the casualty list:

Dead

John Kennan, Leeson Street	Gunshot wound to body	(Catholic Area)
Samuel Baxter, Regent Street	Gunshot wound to chest	(Catholic Area)

Wounded

Patrick Mallon, Kane Street	Gunshot wound to shoulder	(Catholic Area)
John Davey, Frere Street	Gunshot wound to arm	(Catholic Area)
James Conlon, Bow Street	Gunshot wound to leg	(Catholic Area)
Wm. O'Connor, Smithfield	Gunshot wound to arm	(Catholic Area)
John Geegan, Smithfield	Gunshot wound to abdomen	(Catholic Area)
Leo Donnelly, 17 Frere Street	Gunshot wound to arm	(Catholic Area)
James Boyle, address not given	Gunshot wound to leg	(Catholic Area)
James Girvan, Plevna Street	Gunshot wound to abdomen	(Catholic Area)
Daniel McNaughton, Raglan Street	Gunshot wound to hand	(Catholic Area)
Edward Burns, Lepper Street	Gunshot wound to leg	(Catholic Area)
Joseph Magee, Butler Street	Gunshot wound to head & leg	(Catholic Area)
Edmond Sheridan, Gracehill Street	Gunshot wound to head	(Catholic Area)

Terence Burns, Massereene Street	Gunshot wound to back	(Catholic Area)
James Hill, Hanover Street	Gunshot wound to back	(Catholic Area)
Mary Brady, Lincoln Street	Gunshot wound to arm	(Catholic Area)

Injuries

F. Smith, Meadown Street	Injuries to leg and cheek	(Protestant Area)
Stanley Butershill, Conway Street	Injuries to scalp	(Protestant Area)
D. English, North Thomas Street	Cut hands	(Catholic Area)
William Crocker, Eton Street	Lacerated wound to scalp	(Protestant Area)
William Moore, Belgrave Street	Injured hip	(Protestant Area)
Mary Waddell, address not given	Injuries to head	(Protestant Area)
Sergeant Barry, RUC, Court Street	Injuries to leg	(Protestant Area)
Constable Harvey, Lurgan	Wound to head	(Protestant Area)
Constable Foley, Andersonstown	Wound to leg	(Catholic Area)
Sergeant Thompson, Shankill Road	Wound to face	(Protestant Area)
David Gibson, Leopold Street	Injuries to head	(Protestant Area)
John Mackie, Montjoy Street	Injuries to face	(Protestant Area)
Thomas Trainor, Fortingale Street	Fractured skull	(Protestant Area)
Mary Rooney, Upr Library Street	Injuries to hands	(Catholic Area)
Annie Kane, Wilton Street	Lacerated wound to hand	(Protestant Area)
John Robinson, address not given	Injuries to leg	(Protestant Area)
George Hazley, Medway Street	Scalp wound	(Protestant Area)
John Montgomery, Callton Street	Injuries to head	(Protestant Area)
James Moran, Josephine Street	Scalp wound	(Protestant Area)

It was reported that several other persons were treated for injuries in Belfast hospitals but no further information was reported in the newspaper coverage of the riots.[28]

At 3 p.m. on 13 October selected representatives of the Board were called to an urgent meeting at the workhouse to prepare them to meet Cabinet Ministers at Stormont later that afternoon. The meeting was to hear a report from a conference held the previous day between senior members of the Government and officials from the craft unions on the administration of Outdoor Relief payments to able-bodied persons under the Poor Relief (Exceptional Distress) Act 1928. G.B. Hanna, MP, Major G.A. Harris, Permanent Secretary, D.L. Clarke, Assistant Secretary and Vice-Admiral Archdale had represented the Ministry of Home Affairs at the conference. The size and power of this representation indicated that the Government was determined to stand for no further delay on the part of the Guardians and to have the matter settled before a large-scale revolution developed.

Seventeen Belfast Councillors, including ten Official Unionists, were so alarmed by the rioting that they signed a motion for debate in the City Council calling on the Government 'promptly to take such action as may be necessary to relieve distress and starvation amongst the unemployed people of the city'. The motion was signed by J.W. Nixon, MP, M. Mercer, L. McCurdy, R. Byrne, M.P., J. Kilpatrick,

T. Henderson, MP, C.A. Hinds, J. Malcolm, W.J. Chambers, J. Holland, R. Johnston, H. Midgley, W.J. Magowan, Clarke Scott, H. Armstrong, T.L. Cole and D. Lyle Hall.

The Board of Guardians' representatives, according to the Minutes, were told quite bluntly to put before their Board the following scales:

Man and wife	20s. per week
with 1 or 2 children	24s. per week
with 3 or 4 children	28s. per week
with 5 or more children	32s. per week

In granting these scales, account was to be taken of the industrial record of applicants; amounts would be subject to proportionate reductions where there was other income. Moreover, representatives were told that if the strike were settled the men suspended would be kept on relief.[29] Craig himself issued a statement containing news of the proposed new work payments and the family allowances which henceforth were to be applied to recipients.

The terms were voted on and accepted at a mass meeting in St Mary's Hall that Friday night. Tommy Geehan speaking from the platform said that 'A glorious victory had been achieved'. He was quite right. The unemployed workers in every working-class area rejoiced in the victory. The next day one of the men who was shot dead by the police in the lower Falls was buried in Milltown Cemetery. Tens of thousands marched behind the coffin led by Tom Mann, leader of the NUWM. Armoured cars accompanied the cortège and armed police lined the route. At the rates of the cemetery Tom Mann was arrested and taken to a nearby police station.

Tom Mann himself described what happened:

I arrived in Belfast at 6.30 a.m. on Friday morning, Oct. 14th and my first surprise was to see 500 soldiers disembarking and lining up for marching. I had the attention of the 'tecs from the first jump off the boat; they didn't interfere with me in any way during the morning beyond that of following me wherever I went. I joined in the great funeral procession of Comrade Baxter in the afternoon, the other comrade having been buried during the morning. I was by the coffin the whole 2½ hours – the time it took to march through the city, whilst hundreds of thousands lined the sidewalks to the gates of the cemetery. Whilst the funeral ceremony was on, I turned away from the general body to proceed to an important meeting to discuss the arrangements for a big demonstration later in the evening. With the vast crowd unaware of what was happening, I reached the gates of the cemetery; a police detective touched me on the shoulder and said sharply, 'You'll come along with us, Mr Mann.' I said 'What are you – the police?' 'Yes, the police station is only two minutes away. You'll accompany us there and learn what is wanted.'

On arrival at the police station I was informed that I must go at once to police headquarters and that a conveyance was waiting to take me. This conveyance turned out to be an armoured car covered by a bird-cage arrangement. Suffice it to say, this was packed with police, with their revolvers handy and only just enough room left for me. At police headquarters I was told by the Chief Superintendent that he was responsible for my arrest and that a deportation would follow. He asked 'Was it your intention to hold public meetings?' I said it certainly was, and that I was intending to hold a meeting at the Custom House steps on Sunday night. He then said that would be impossible as they could not allow such a gathering. A long talk ensued, but it finished by my being handed an expulsion order to be operated forthwith. This was at 5.30 p.m. and at 8.30 the same evening I was taken in a car to the boat which left at 9.15.[30]

The workers returned to work on Monday, 17 October. On Tuesday, 18 October the Chairman of the Guardians issued a statement commenting on newspaper coverage of the strike in which he said that the increased scales were not granted because of pressure from the Outdoor Relief strikers, but because of his Committee's efforts earlier that year. Collins and Diamond were not impressed and at the Board meeting on 19 October told him that the increases were brought about only after blood had been shed and the city turned into a shambles by the Guardians. Eight days afterwards the curfew was lifted and the city returned to normal.[31]

Six hundred new applications for relief were received within the next few days. A special committee of the Board which met on 19 October reported on the increased number of applications and asked the Ministry of Home Affairs to agree to a tentative scheme to open up new premises to deal with them. They had in mind a main office located centrally and four district offices.[32]

It was intended that the central office would contain the supervisor, assistant supervisor, two general assistants and two pay-out clerks. Each district office would consist of one clerk and three to four investigators. The duty of each clerk was to issue forms, receive them at stated times and return them to the central office where they would be examined by a supervisor. Investigators were to interview applicants in their own homes and submit reports to the central office. Relief for each case would be determined by the supervisor for a fixed period in line with instructions he would receive from the Board. Payments would be made on the same day each week. The supervisor or his assistant would consider all cases and if necessary interview applicants personally. Only in cases of doubt would there be a referral to the Board. However the supervisor would be required to report weekly to the Board on the financial provisions made by him.

Supervisory staff would be seconded from the Civil Service and general assistants recruited locally. A new system of payment by cheque or paying order to replace grocers' chits was to be established. Hours of business would commence each morning from 9.30 and conclude at 5.30 p.m., except on Saturday when they would end at 1 p.m.

Mr John E. Barry was appointed supervisor at an annual salary of £550. He had served in the Civil Service for many years and had wide experienced in administrative affairs. Barry took over immediately and made arrangements, because of the backlog of applications to process, to open new district offices on 12 December 1932. He made the suggestion, to which the Board agreed, that payments be made at the district offices as well as the central office.

Six offices were put into operation:

Central Office	James Street South
No. 1 & 5 Districts	North Queen Street
No. 2	Runford Street
No. 3 & 3A	Glengall Street
No. 4	Springfield Road
No. 1 & 2 (Down)	Templemore Avenue

The changes came not a moment too soon. The pressure on the new officials was inexorable. The volume of demand had increased in the numbers of applicants and in the scale of need. The following information gives some indication of this scale.

29 October 3870 cases involving 16,365 people

Wages paid out for week ending 29th October: £1,369.7.9.
Total days worked: 3286
Total men engaged: 1241

15 November 4302 cases involving 17,539 people

Wages paid out for week ending 15th November: £1,622.7.9.
Total days worked: 4036
Total men engaged: 1497 [33]

In less than six weeks reforms to the organisation had generated an increase of 20 per cent in Outdoor Relief payments. This was certainly needed to assuage the ugly mood of the unemployed workers of Belfat who were conscious of the power of their collective anger against a Poor Law system that could have treated them with more humanity earlier if their own Government and Guardians had so willed.

Belfast newspapers reported on 16 December that 900 men, who had been waiting to be paid out at the central office from early morning, began to riot because of delay in payment. Police had to be called to control them. The following day 750 men who were paid out at the same office were treated with more respect. Obviously directions had been sent by the Ministry of Home Affairs to the central office to avoid further eruptions involving recipients.

Ill-temper was not confined to the unemployed. The Guardians were furious that they had been disregarded by the Government in working out the solution that gave the Outdoor Relief workers twice the rate they themselves had been granting. They felt humiliated by the Government giving in to the paupers and had advocated that the riot be put down by force. They were bitter also because the changes imposed on them had transferred a considerable number of their duties and responsibilities into the hands of the new supervisor. They reckoned as well that more of their power and authority was being filched from them by Vice-Admiral Archdale's presence at their meetings and his insistence on their following Ministerial policies.

Parliament re-opened with the usual ritual on 22 November 1932. Professor Corkey, MP, moving a vote of thanks to the King's Address, congratulated the Government and the Churches on taking away the leadership of the movement from those agitating for reform of the Outdoor Relief administration. 'Whole credit', he said, 'must go to the Government for lending an ear to the complaints of those people and for interpreting their needs in a reasonable way'.[34]

Jack Beattie, speaking later in the same debate, said that he was proud to be an agitator who had forced the Government into doing its duty to feed the hungry, that he was not satisfied with crumbs off the table for his class and that the spirit of the new arrangement was the same as the old one.

The *Manchester Guardian* carried an editorial on October 14 that had more than a prophetic ring to it:

> It is one of the paradoxes of Northern Ireland that the maintenance of an old religious and political feud has prevented the development of what by economic conditions, temperament and tradition is almost naturally a revolutionary urban proletariat.

This was also the view of Sir Wilfrid Spender, who recorded in his diary (9 January 1934) that the Outdoor Relief riots had been the most significant moment of proletarian unity in Belfast since 1921. He described the agitation as 'so serious that wilful damage could quite easily have been greater than the £300,000 spent on relief schemes'.

Events, however, had proved Bates right in his assessment of what would happen if riots developed in Belfast. His police force had been put under enormous pressure from the working classes of North, East and West Belfast – until they were rescued by the Cabinet's decisions to pay out £300,000 to fund a new set of relief schemes which involved doubling the relief payments to the able-bodied destitute. The Cabinet, including the anti-populists, were relieved that they had got off so lightly when they saw the size of the anti-Government forces that confronted the police on the streets of Belfast.

The Government were acutely aware of the situation in which they found themselves. By their own folly in ignoring the Guardians' capacity for making trouble until it was nearly too late, pushing labour representatives on to the streets in 1929 in political protest against undesirable aspects of their administration, they had imperilled their own strategy. They recognised too, when the smoke had blown away, the absolute necessity of returning immediately to the sectarian tactics of the early Twenties or of finding a new set of instruments to reassert control over the situation. As it happened they were to try both.

9

The Aftermath of the Riots

The Outdoor Relief riots in Belfast were inevitable because of the Poor Law Guardians' rigid attitude towards the poor of the city and because of the Government's failure to protect the political rights of its Parliamentary Opposition and the social rights of the Catholic minority.

Both attitudes were entirely typical of their administrators. Only the best was good enough for their own supporters. Every opportunity was taken to repress even further the anti-Unionists who chose to remain in Northern Ireland after 1920. Additional hardships beyond those normally created by the harsh economic laws of the capitalist system were inflicted, imposed by a so-called democratic government that confined its ideas of democracy to the majority of votes recorded without regard to other democratic essentials.

Considerable changes had taken place in the administration of Outdoor Relief in the wake of the riots of 1932. Unionists in Belfast were taken by surprise that rioting against their own institutions could take place with the participation of their own working-class supporters. The blame was placed almost entirely on the Poor Law Guardians because of their failure to respond to the Government's suggestions to treat the poor more humanely and to stretch out with their relief facilities to the supporters of the Government amongst the City's destitute. It was not the Government's intention that the Guardians should behave so insensitively to their party supporters.

Bates had seen the storm coming. He had seen at an early stage the potential dangers to their strategy and had moved his 'mafia', headed now by Archdale, to pre-empt working-class anger exploding against the Guardians. His manoeuvre failed because the Guardians in their arrogance believed they knew better how to treat the destitute, than did the officials of the Ministry of Home Affairs. More important to Bates than the Guardians' arrogance was the absence of any party organisation in the riot areas which could stop this type of upheaval developing again. For example, in 1920, the Unionists, under Lord Carson's guiding hand, were able to organise bands of sectarian mercenaries to act when necessary in these areas. The action taken then succeeded in dividing Catholic and Protestant workers who had united in common cause or interest against employers. It had not happened this time. The Guardians by their vulgar excesses had united the workers solidly; so much so, that even their traditional supporters in the Ulster Unionist Labour Association were unsympathetic to the Unionist Poor Law Guardians. There was no working-class organisation on the Unionist side willing to carry out a campaign against Catholics as they had done in the past. Moreover the Unionists in Parliament, like William Grant and John F. Gordon, had lost contact with local organisations and were unable to give front-line leadership to this type of activity as Grant had done in 1920 when he had worked in the shipyard. Nevertheless, within days of the riots ending, they succeeded in establishing the Ulster Protestant League.

The political tenor of this organisation was evident in their first public statement on the Outdoor Relief Strike issued on 15 October.

> We deplore that these unfortunate conditions were used as a cloak by the Communist Sinn Fein element to attempt to start a revolution in our province. We also greatly deplore that some of our loyal Protestant unemployed were misled to such an extent that they associated themselves with enemies of their faith and principles. We congratulate the Government of Northern Ireland on the firm steps that they have taken to preserve law and order in our City.[1]

It soon emerged that the stated objective of the UPL differed widely from its real objective. Immediately after its formation it set out aggressively to safeguard the employment of Protestants; stating that its members were prepared 'neither to talk with, nor to walk with, neither to buy or sell, borrow or lend, take or give or have any dealings with them [Catholics] at all, nor for employers to employ nor employees to work with Catholics'.[2]

The UPL immediately became active in the areas of Court and Dock Wards where the bonds of friendship formed during the riots were strongest. Leading Unionist MPs gave them public support in their efforts to stoke up sectarian fires. Two of these leaders were convicted of charges of incitement to disorder; one of them had exhorted

138

supporters 'to get training in firing'.[3]

Party contact with the UPL was set up by the Chief Whip, Sir Daniel Dixon, who had a builders' supply business in the Docks area and was able to reach this organisation through workers in the family firm who were members. He had done so in August 1932 when the Unionists had exhorted them to attack Catholics in the hope that the ensuing publicity could be used at Westminster to lift the pressure off the Ulster Government to have the 'B' Special Constabulary reduced in strength. Dixon in a letter to Sir Wilfrid Spender claimed that he had settled the Protestant activists in the area and persuaded them against becoming a grave danger. The implication in the letter was that attacks on Catholics would be limited to the point that Westminster would be impressed only enough to keep the 'B' Specials on patrol duties.

Craig sought to realign his supporters in a public statement made immediately after the riots: 'Ours is a Protestant Government and I am an Orangeman'.[4] Later he elaborated:

I have always said I am an Orangeman first and a politician and member of this Parliament afterwards... All I boast is that we are a Protestant Parliament and a Protestant State. Therefore, it is undoubtedly our duty and our privilege, and always will be, to see that those appointed by us possess the most unimpeachable loyalty to the King and Constitution. This is my whole object in carrying on a Protestant Government for a Protestant people.[5]

Speeches on this theme from leading Unionist and Orange leaders became more frequent in the days that followed. Nine months afterwards Sir Basil Brooke, who was later to become Prime Minister, said at an Orange demonstration that he had not a Roman Catholic about his place. His statement, when challenged later by Joseph Devlin in Parliament, brought forth a flow of praise from Craig who supported categorically his Cabinet Minister's stand.[6]

Another MP, Major J.A. McCormick, defined the strategy in precise terms on the same Orange platform as Brooke:

Thousands of Roman Catholics had been added to the population either by birth rate or the adoption of this province as their home. In many places Protestant majorities were now minorities and at that rate of increase twenty years would see the Church of Rome in power. Instead of waiting and telling them to get out means should be taken to prevent them from coming in.[7]

Six weeks later, at another Orange demonstration, Sir Joseph Davison, Grand Master of the Orange Order, tried his hand. He asked the assembled Orangemen,

> when will the Protestant employers of Northern Ireland recognise their duty to their Protestant brothers and sisters and employ them to the exclusion of Roman Catholics. It is time Protestant employers realised that whenever a Roman Catholic is brought into their employment it means one Protestant vote less. It is our duty to pass the word along from this great demonstration and I suggest the slogan should be 'Protestants employ Protestants'.[8]

Craig realised as well that he had to realign the Party's working-class support with Unionist policy and the overall strategy. He had seen how that support had been driven away on simple class issues to which the petit bourgeoisie in the Party had been so insensitive. Having watched Lord Carson at work after the First World War when he used the Ulster Unionist Labour Association to destroy the labour movement by infiltration, he could see no reason for changing the tactics. Accordingly he set out to woo the UULA back into line with favourable public statements about them, and a generous set of public works and relief projects. He praised them first as a very representative body, more important even than the Orange Order. He was challenged on this statement by Sir Joseph Davidson, Grand Master of the Orange Order, and replied most fulsomely on 12 January 1933, saying that 'the UULA were the most wonderful organisation in Ulster, containing the cream of our working classes and so many influential trade union leaders'. It was quite true that the UULA and the trade unions – there was a heavy dual membership – formed the power base of the Unionist Party; many were in the Orange Order as well.

Andrews was persuaded by Craig to use more trade union officials on the various consultative bodies and appeals committees under his control. He admitted in Parliament that he had consulted trade union officials on matters pertaining to the running of his Ministery – not as strange an admission as at first it sounds because he had become president of the UULA after Carson's death.

The speeches of Craig and his colleagues after 1932, aimed at creating hysteria amongst Unionists, were not without a certain amount of substance. The IRA had come alive meanwhile, to assist strikers against the railway employers in the North, when their bosses had ꞁut wages in January 1933. It seemed like a straightforward confrontation between the employees, most of whom were Protestant, and the railway owners. Several of the railway company directors were Cabinet Ministers, and Bates was their legal adviser. (Bates enjoyed a privileged relationship with the railways. Each Monday morning he caught a train from Portrush, where he lived, to Belfast – the 'Bates Special', arranged to suit his personal needs.) The confrontation became a very violent strike, taking on the characteristics of a fierce class war. The Unions supported the railway workers since they saw the attempt to reduce the wages as the 'thin end of the wedge' which would in time be extended to other industrial workers.

Blacklegs were employed on a massive scale to keep the trains running. They were installed in the best hotels in Belfast and paid £4 10.0. per week – the railway workers when working receiving only £2. The blacklegs consisted of the staff and management of the railways supplemented by Queen's University students. RUC men operated signal boxes and worked as porters, presumably under directions from Bates.

The IRA in Belfast took a hand, prompted by left-wing leaders in Dublin led by Peader O'Donnell. They set off bombs under bridges, threw hand grenades at railway property and fired shots at blacklegs, finally shooting dead a policeman on guard at a goods yard in Belfast.

The Revolutionary Workers' Group, too, had seen the opportunity presented by the Outdoor Relief riots and the railway strikes and tried to broaden it into a general political conflict on a class basis.

Billie McMullen, by this time a leading officer of the Irish Transport and General Workers Union, returned from Dublin to lead a torch-light procession of 5,000 union members from Belfast City Hall to the Custom House steps. Speaking at the subsequent meeting, he said, 'We don't care about governments. The industrial army and the working class have only to remain passive and the wheels of industry will cease.'9

McMullen's presence in Dublin had coincided with a stronger line being advocated by Peader O'Donnell in his editorials on class issues which were published in the IRA newspaper, *An Phoblacht*. Left-wing members of the IRA council were pushing for a programme of Socialist reconstruction as a means of earning popular support for their aims. Resistance to the programme by right-wingers led to a group of prominent IRA men issuing a public statement on 7 April 1934:

We believe that a Republic or a United Ireland will never be achieved except through a struggle which uproots capitalism on its way. We cannot conceive of a free Ireland with a subject working class: we cannot conceive of a subject Ireland with a free working class.

Arising from this trade unionists in Dublin and Belfast issued a statement calling for support for a proposed Republican Congress. Congress committees were set up in Belfast and Dublin and the Republican Congress of 23 June 1934, commenting on the situation in Belfast, stated:

> Sectarianism dies slowly when the fight against it is one of words. Sectarianism burns out quickly when there is team work in the common struggle. Those who see in partition just a reflex of sectarian strife can see no way forward except in soft, foolish talk about toleration, charity, real religion, etc. Those who see in partition the link between Irish capitalism and Imperialist finance, however, see in the common struggle for the Workers' Republic the solution of partition and in the destruction of exploitation the withering of sectarian strife.[10]

Three buses carrying trade unionists and unemployed from the Shankill Road arrived at the Wolfe Tone commemoration ceremony at Bodenstown. They carried a banner to the graveside which stated, 'Break the connection with Capitalism'. Some of those in attendance were not unduly enthusiastic and made an attempt to attack them but were restrained: the Congress met in Rathmines Town Hall at the end of September. One hundred and eighty-six delegates attended, thirty of whom were from the North, and Billie McMullen presided.

Though a split developed between the two groups, represented by Peader O'Donnell on the one hand and Michael Price on the other, it was quite clear that the Republican Congress was to be a revolutionary Republican organisation with the declared aim of uniting Catholic and Protestant, North and South, in an attack on the capitalist system in every sphere of its operation. This development appeared to be a perfect justification of Craig's action after the riots in 1932, when he put the Special Powers Act permanently on the Statute Book in 1933. He made full use of these incidents and the affairs of the Republican Congress in a series of attempts to drive the Protestant working class away from their Catholic fellow workers. He had concluded that the only way to do it was to blow apart the newly-forged unity between

Catholic and Protestant unemployed. But the explosion that would destroy the unity of the unemployed had a longer fuse this time and was slower to detonate. The forging of that unity was too recent in their minds for them to go out and kill one another at the bidding of Unionist politicians.

By 1935, the Unionist Party had recovered its position in the working-class areas, and was again able to influence events in ways that suited their strategy. Riots returned to inner Belfast, and before they were finished, 500 Catholic families had been driven from their homes, hundreds of people suffered gunshot wounds or injuries and thirteen people were killed.

It was no surprise to find that before tranquility returned to these areas the two halls most extensively used by the Outdoor Relief workers as food centres during the strike were gutted by fires which were 'mysteriously started'.

Harry Midgley, who had been elected to the Northern Ireland Parliament in 1933 for the Dock Constituency, was strangely silent about the rioting which was patently incited by Unionist politicians who had paid local thugs to attack Catholic traders in the area. One of these thugs, a well-known boxer who became converted to the labour cause twenty years later, admitted to being paid by William Grant for taking a leading part in the attacks.

Midgley was aware that he would always get the Catholic vote in the Dock area for it was virulently anti-Unionist and would probably support him at the polls in any case. To win the seat he had to have Protestant working-class support. Rather than risk alienating that support which was shaky he made no condemnation of the attacks on the Catholic residents of Dock.

Of course, Midgley's leadership of the Northern Ireland Labour Party developed along different lines from those of his predecessors of the Twenties. Beattie, still in Parliament, had been expelled from the Party for refusing to move the election writ, as instructed by the party, for Devlin's seat when he died in 1934. McMullen and Kyle had gone to take up senior union appointments.

Midgley, left virtually on his own, persuaded the Party to change the emphasis as well as the issues of party policies. By the middle Thirties the Party swung away from its anti-partition position into a pro-partition one; concentrating less on issues of unemployment and destitution which had led to street demonstrations and riots of 1932, than on the more 'respectable' political exchanges of the Stormont Parliament.

East and West Belfast meanwhile were storm centres of rampaging Unionist mobs that roamed the streets attacking isolated Catholic families and traders. The violence, which had been whipped up gradually by Unionist politicians, came alive in serious proportions on the day of the Jubilee Celebrations for King George V. A number of Catholics were shot and bombs were thrown into Catholic areas. At the inquest held afterwards on those who were killed, the Belfast Coroner said:

Party passion is a very inflammable commodity, bigotry is the curse of peace and goodwill. The poor people who commit these riots are easily led and influenced... They are influenced almost entirely by the public speeches of men in high and responsible positions. There would be less bigotry if there were less public speech-making by so-called leaders of public opinion... It is not good Protestantism to preach a gospel of hate and enmity towards those who differ from us in religion and politics.[12]

The riots attracted wide publicity outside Northern Ireland. English journalists were quickly on the scene and reported in detail the consequences of the violence. This publicity caused Unionist leaders acute embarrassment. They were now in government, unlike 1920, and had an obligation to protect Catholics from rioting mobs.

On 13 July the *Manchester Guardian* published an editorial which included the following comment:

Craig's Government has been continuously in power since 1921. The circumstances in which it came into power explain why it then adopted the theory and technique of the "one party style" regarding its political opponents as intending rebels and basing its power on the Orange Order. That may have been necessary in 1921. If so, it was at best an ugly necessity.

There was, thus, the temptation to presume that every Catholic was disloyal until the contrary was proved, to base the state on the principle of a Protestant ascendancy and to strengthen the position of the Government and its one party state by stimulating the anti-Catholic bigotry of all sections of the population especially the least enlightened... There has been too much talk of a Protestant government for a Protestant people.

The point was well made and by no means lost on the Government. Police were drafted in from country areas and posted at flash points to prevent any further outbreaks of violence. It was beginning to dawn on the Unionists that the weapon of rioting had less usefulness for them while they were in power than it had in the nineteenth century when they were a minority party. There were more sophisticated ways of securing the same aims as long as the levels of institutional power remained in their hands.

The *Manchester Guardian* had accurately evaluated the Unionist Government's position on the riots. While in government, on Westminster's terms, they had to give the appearance of observing Westminster's standards on matters of public order. Large-scale rioting with its corresponding publicity was embarrassing to the British Government to whom the growing Irish vote in the major cities of Britain was becoming a factor in maintaining power. Coupled with this, it could do only harm to Britain's relations with her European and American friends.

Nonetheless, the results sought by the Unionist Government had been achieved in spite of the difficulties. What were those results? They were: firstly, that the mainly Protestant skilled workers were either at work, having first call on all jobs or were receiving benefit or relief from government sources and therefore were still well disposed to the Unionist Party and secondly, that the unemployed were split into two factions, Catholic and Protestant, and were unlikely to come together again to confront the Government as they had done in 1932.

Their strategy was safe once again.

10
Old Wine, New Bottles

The Unionists in government had not the same freedom of tactics that they had enjoyed before 1921. They learned from experience that the tactic of using riots to control the growth of their political opponents was counterproductive and their dependence on the Poor Law Guardians adhering to their strategical requirements was no longer a wise or sound proposition.

They had to find a new set of tactics, more subtle, effective and covert, to achieve their aims. As the legitimately elected Government they could invoke the due processes and agencies of the state to pursue their objectives, and this included the use of statutory provision for Outdoor Relief. However, this involved the risk of having to accept the power of the Poor Law Guardians to administer that relief.

It was a prospect the Government did not relish. Parliamentary Reports for the period make it clear that the Government had made up its mind to use the parliamentary process to amend Westminster legislation to suit its objectives. In following this approach they were reducing the risk of the Guardians destroying their strategy. They began to transfer the implementation of this legislation to civil servants who they felt were more capable of achieving their political purpose.

But the Guardians were not yet out of the picture. In retaliation for their setback over the 1932 riots, they refused to meet the Outdoor Relief workers on the matter of paying wages for time lost due to inclement weather. Tom Geehan, who had written to the Guardians in the first instance, contacted Beattie who then raised the matter with the Minister of Home Affairs after which a meeting was arranged with the Advisory Committee of the Board.[1]

The meeting was held with the Committee on 17 February 1933. Vice-Admiral Archdale attended to hear the delegation's submissions. Geehan said that the workers should not lose a day's pay because of rain. He claimed that the agreement made between workers and Guardians the previous October protected them against this type of loss. The Guardians replied that they had made no agreement with the workers. The delegation in reply offered to work an extra half day on Saturday to recover part of the loss of one day's pay from the week before, but the Guardians replied that the books were closed and could not be opened again. When the delegation left the decision not to yield on the matter was confirmed by motion.

The Guardians should have complied with the agreement made by Bates and Craig with the Outdoor Relief strikers, but to show their resentment at their treatment by the Government they refused to honour the agreement or to respond to the compromise offered by Geehan on the Relief Workers' behalf.

The following morning men working on one of the schemes in Dundee Street stopped work as a token protest on hearing of the decision not to pay wages during wet weather. When they returned to work after lunch they were sent home until the following morning on direct instructions from the Guardians.[2] Geehan, hearing of this incident, again wrote to the Guardians on 14 March 1933. He received an immediate reply informing him that the Guardians wanted no further communications from him as they did not recognise his organisation. On 28 March a delegation led by Geehan turned up at the locked gates of the workhouse and asked to be received by the Guardians to discuss their refusal to pay 'wet-time'. They were turned away from the gate by police.

No effective protest following the Guardians' abrupt refusal to meet the Unemployed Workers' Movement was noted in public records or newspaper reports, although in Great Britain wholesale demonstrations and hunger marches were increasingly commanding attention. This would seem to indicate that Unionist tactics to disengage unemployed Unionist workers from the orthodox class struggles were even then beginning to work.

Inside the Poor Law boardroom, Harry Diamond, who was incessantly active on behalf of the able-bodied unemployed, raised the matter of single men not being considered for relief – an issue which was understood to be part of the October agreement. The Board asserted that their policy had not changed in this regard.

Diamond was far from satisfied with this reply, being determined to bring the rigid attitude of the Guardians into the open. At a Board meeting on 20 June 1933 he moved that the test for investigating applicants' means before granting relief be abolished. The Chairman, Mrs Lily Coleman, ruled the motion out of order even though notice had been properly given a fortnight before. Several other members wished to speak but were told to keep quiet and Diamond was ordered to sit down. Diamond reacted angrily by throwing a doormat at Mrs Coleman. Police were called in, and Diamond and two other Catholic Guardians were ejected from the meeting.[3] This incident did not have any lasting effect and the issue of the Guardians' treatment of the Outdoor Relief workers sank gradually into oblivion.

The following year, a change did occur that helped recipients of relief outside the category of the able-bodied unemployed. This was announced at a special meeting of the Board which was convened on 20 March 1934; Vice-Admiral Archdale was in attendance. The Minutes of the meeting suggest that it was forced on the Guardians by the intervention of the Unionist Party hierarchy. The Clerk informed the Board that it had been recommended by the Local Government Commission that all relief granted on discretion should be paid in cash in the same manner as local government applied it across the water. It was decided to postpone the matter until the next meeting and that J. Thompson, a Unionist Guardian, would move that relief in kind be replaced by cash grants.

A meeting was convened for 9 April 1934 specifically to enable Thompson to put his motion. A delegation to oppose the motion and a letter in support were received. Mr W.A. Stitt, representing the Grocers' Section of the Private Traders Mutual Development Association, said that it was their duty to protest against the Board stopping relief dockets.

> It was a slur on decent legitimate grocers who could be trusted to give an honest and true return of the quantities of groceries supplied by him. He believed that a percentage of dockets did find their way into the hands of a few unscrupulous traders but in view of the prevalency of gambling amongst the poor, to suspend the granting of relief dockets for cash payments would be a fatal error.[4]

The Irish Co-operative Women's Guild wrote, with more charity, recording their pleasure at the changeover of relief in kind to relief in cash. The motion was passed unanimously recommending that the change should take place on 1 May 1934.[5]

On 29 May 1934 the Minister of Labour introduced a new Unemployment Bill, which was to have widespread effect on the operation of the Poor Law. The Bill had three main clauses: it was to replace the Unemployment Insurance Act, dealing with all unemployment claims to statutory benefits; it was an entirely new scheme to deal with all claimants who exhausted their statutory benefit and all able-bodied persons in receipt of poor relief; it provided for the appointment of an unemployment insurance commission to enquire into the working of the Act to make recommendations every year as to changes in amounts of benefits, of contributions or in administration.

In his introduction to the Bill, Andrews said:

> The Poor Law had long been recognised as an inappropriate medium of relief for able-bodied industrial workers who were unemployed through causes beyond their control. [Cheers recorded in House of Parliament.] In future such aid will come from fellow men as well as ratepayers: a new non-contributory fund for Unemployment Assistance will be established: tax-payers paying 95 per cent and ratepayers 5 per cent to be paid to unemployed residents of United Kingdom for 5 years who ordinarily work in the industrial field: it was intended to cover an extra 100,000 people who had not been able to secure employment: age limit 16–65. The amount of allowance would be determined by reference to unemployed's needs, including members of Household depending on breadwinners: there would be a right of appeal to Tribunals: fulfillment of definite rights to fixed benefits under categories defined by statute.[6]

The Act laid down a common level of financial aid to all recipients, varied according to the size of families. The payments were to be extracted from taxes and administered by an Unemployment Assistance Board.

Two stages of procedure would be established. One was to be known as the 'First Appointed Day', the other as the 'Second Appointed Day'. The first stage was to cover all unemployed receiving state benefit; the second to cover all those outside the scope of unemployment insurance schemes, whose only resources had been the Poor Law.

The Guardians received a letter from the Minister of Labour on 7 June regarding uncovenanted or transitional payments to the able-bodied under the terms of the Bill. Anticipating that it would be carried on to the Statute Book, the following payments would operate from 1 July 1934:

	Old Rate s. d.	New Rate s. d.
Men aged 21 upwards	15 3	17 0
Men aged 18 under 21	12 6	14 0
Women aged 21 upwards	13 6	15 0
Women aged 18 under 21	10 9	12 0
Adult dependent	8 0	9 0
Child	2 0	2 0

A similar Bill had been drafted in Britain to remove unemployment assistance from the political arena. This issue had been subject to radical change of treatment depending on the party in power. Had the Stormont Government applied it without change to Northern Ireland then their strategy would have been finished. But Andrews, in his speech introducing the Bill, outlined their determination to maintain their discretionary power in providing relief.

Throughout the North in every workhouse area, including Belfast, these Boards were effective instruments in applying Unionist strategy. It was clear, in spite of Andrews' observations, that he was not proposing to take action similar to that being taken in Britain to grant fixed benefits by statute to the unemployed, the incapacitated and the destitute. He had seen to it that it was amended to apply differently to Northern Ireland.

Harry Midgley, replying for the Opposition, attempted to tease out Andrews' real intentions, and said that the Bill would perpetuate the means test and still divide recipients into classes; those who had a good insurance record and those who had not. He asked Andrews would they still be subject to refusal on the basis of 'not genuinely seeking work' or 'not normally in insurable employment'?

Midgley was referring to the use and existence of the dreaded means test for political and religious identification, and to the two conditions for disqualification from benefit and relief which were to be used by the Public Assistance Committee.

It was the use of these two conditions and others not explicit that enabled insurance officers and tribunal officials to select who should receive benefits. Applicants were successful if they were tradesmen or at some time or another had been employed in an engineering firm. They were invariably unsuccessful if they had no employment record in that industry. If that arrangement did not deny benefit to the non-Unionist unemployed, then they could be refused on the condition they were not 'genuinely seeking work'. The decision on this condition usually rested on one's employment record. Constant employment in the past, of which few Catholics could boast, was the sole arbiter. Hence when the Government did get around to applying the provisions of the Unemployment Act, the numbers covered were not 100,000 as referred to in the Minister's speech but a mere fraction of that number.

The Act was passed but was not implemented for reasons known only to the Government. They had the parliamentary majority to put it through its various stages as quickly as they wanted. The delay was doubtless inspired by a desire on their part to use it in a way that would not disturb the arrangements for preserving their strategic objectives.

On 3 January 1935 a further letter was sent to the Guardians from the Minister of Labour which stated that under the Unemployment Act (NI) 1934 an order had been made which set up 7 January 1935 as the 'First Appointed Day' and 1 March 1935 as the 'Second Appointed Day' of the two-stage procedure for introducing the new Act. The letter also stated that the Unemployment Insurance (Transitional Payments) Regulations (Northern Ireland) 1931 would cease from 7 January 1935.[7]

The old Transitional Board consisting entirely of Unionists and their camp followers met to wind up its affairs as directed by the Act. It was revealed in a public statement that £1¼ million was spent on 220,000 cases since its formation in 1931. The meeting concluded after the members who felt they had done a patriotic duty had risen to their feet to sing the National Anthem.

The Ministry of Labour's plans for the 'Second Appointed Day' were, however, coming adrift. The Ministry wrote to the Guardians on 25 February 1935 to tell them that they were not in a position to implement the second part of the Act until further notice but required the Guardians to continue with the current arrangements for relief.[8]

Wilson, and indeed the Guardians as a whole, were not slow to follow up the Government's letter. Almost immediately it became the main theme of each succeeding meeting of the Board. On 29 March 1935 a resolution of the Board was sent to the Government reminding them that the Guardians were still providing relief for able-bodied unemployed and that it was costing eleven pence in the pound of rateable value to provide that relief. The Government replied on 15 April 1935 that they were aware of the problem and had it under discussion with other local authorities. This statement was patently untrue. What was true, however, was that some delay was being caused in England because the new central scale of rates was not as high as those already being paid by some local authorities. In Northern Ireland, however, no such inhibitions existed – the lowest rate would be paid without protest.

At the annual meeting of the Board on 6 June 1935 Anastasia McCready, JP (Chairman of the Board), said it was a matter of regret that there was still heavy weekly expenditure under the Poor Relief (Exceptional Distress) Act 1928. There had not been any distress work schemes in operation for some time nor any return received for money paid as relief to able-bodied unemployed. Miss McCready's sentiments were echoed by her colleagues frequently in the following days: her sentiments were translated into the Board's treatment of the increasing number of cases.

It was quite obvious that the public expression of these views by the Board's leading members was completely in line with the practical application of their relief scales. The first six months' figures showed an increase in the number of applicants and a reduction in the amount of money spent per head. This trend was allowed to continue in spite of the rates specified by the Minister of Labour in his letter to the Guardians in June of the previous year.

The following figures are an example of the meanness of that application:

8 January 1935	2,594 cases received in total payments	£4399. 0. 6.
8 February 1935	2,722 cases received in total payments	£4440. 0. 6.
9 March 1935	2,821 cases received in total payments	£4433. 0. 6.
6 April 1935	2,906 cases received in total payments	£4371.11. 0.
4 May 1935	2,979 cases received in total payments	£4470.18. 0.
8 June 1935	3,078 cases received in total payments	£4168.15. 6. [9]

Suspicion was aroused in the minds of the Opposition by the Government's procrastination in implementing the 'Second Appointed Day'. The Government had declared already its readiness to extend a system of cash benefits similar to that which was made available to the able-bodied unemployed by local authorities in Great Britain. The machinery was in operation for the first part of the exercise. To extend benefit to the extra people on the 'Second Appointed Day' would be a fairly simple process. But in Northern

Ireland, there was an important reason for the delay.

As far back as December 1934 in a series of parliamentary questions, Beattie and Midgley produced in one of the answers information that the Unemployment Assistance Committee was to have complete discretion in fixing the amounts of relief as long as they did not exceed those laid down by the Transitional Payments (Determination of Need) Act 1932 and that their application would be varied from area to area.

At the Second Reading of the Bill, the Parliamentary Secretary to the Minister of Labour said that its object was to restore cuts in transitional payments and to continue to pay any increase to applicants determined by the Unemployment Assistance Board. 'The Bill, when passed,' he stated, 'would be built on top of the Unemployment Assistance Act 1934 and would provide that no one would have the right to appeal to a Tribunal except by leave of the Chairman of the Board who of course would be appointed by the Minister.' The Parliamentary Secretary went on to explain that powers would be given to the Board to enable them to add a supplementary allowance based on Board officials' assessment of need.[9] The Chairman was a political appointment whose responsibility it was to see that interpretation of the Act in Northern Ireland conformed to the strategic requirements of the Government.

Jack Beattie retorted that the Government was not keeping in step with Britain on the application of the 1934 Act.

> Power was given under the British Act to Public Health Authorities to administer to poor as a right. In Northern Ireland it was still given to the harsh and cruel Poor Law Guardians to apply at their discretion.

Harry Midgley referred to a case in Manchester in which a father was charged and convicted for not claiming full allowances for his family. The prosecution had been initiated by the Public Assistance Committee. (The differences here were irreconcilable.)[10]

The Minister of Labour, speaking on his department's estimates on 30 May 1935, said that the scheme embraced 260,000 persons on 1 January 1935 and another 100,000 would be included on the 'Second Appointed Day'. The scheme would apply to all persons normally obtaining a living through gainful employment. The cost of the scheme would be £425,000 per annum and staff costs would be in the region of 7¾ per cent. It did seem strange with that amount of information in the

Minister's possession that it took him such an extraordinarily long time to bring forward the 'Second Appointed Day'.

Obviously, private talks on the matter had taken place in Unionist Party Headquarters on the most advantageous way in which to handle the delay. It was as a result of these talks that a letter was sent from the Ministry to the Guardians several weeks later to inform them that an Exchequer grant equal to the amount paid out, as if the 'Second Appointed Day' had not been postponed, would be paid to them. This arrangement it was claimed would serve the ratepayers of Belfast much better.

The Government was not yet out of the fire, because the trend of more applications and diminishing relief payments was in evidence in the figures for the early months of 1936.

		Total weekly payments
8 February 1936	3,752 cases received	£3562. 15. 0.
7 March 1936	3,829 cases received	£3344. 19. 6.
4 April 1936	3,903 cases received	£3424. 16. 1.
2 May 1936	3,993 cases received	£3252. 13. 0.
6 June 1936	4,113 cases received	£3027. 17. 1.

The matter of reductions in relief payments had not escaped the attention of the Opposition MPs at a time when the Government had promised improvements during the debates which accompanied the passage of the Unemployment Act in 1935. Beattie, speaking on the adjournment debate on 1 April 1936, accused them of reneguing on their promise that provision for the able-bodied unemployed would be taken out of the hands of the Guardians and given to the Public Assistance Board. The Minister said in reply that he would attempt to remedy injustices even though he had only limited powers in the situation.[11]

Later that year, on 26 October, J.R. Campbell, MP, leader of the Irish Nationalists since the death of Joseph Devlin, moved an amendment to the Unemployment Assistance (Determination of Need) Regulation to the effect that 'this House regrets that the regulations in many cases will lower the already low allowance of the Unemployed, will fail to maintain the unemployed and dependants in health and fitness.'

In the course of his speech, Campbell said: 'The Regulation bristled with injustices; it did not give working-class people comfort and subsistence and was harsh towards the large number of people who seldom get good food or good clothing.' He went on to quote a statement from the British Medical Association in 1933 which stated that it took 6s. per week to pay for the minimum food requisite for a human being: the Minister proposed to pay only half that amount. Breaking down the figure to cover items of necessary expense, Campbell said that 'there was only 8s. left for clothes, recreation, and saving for marriage of young men over 21, therefore, marriage was ruled out'. 'Was this the intention?' he asked.[12]

The Opposition were not disenchanted with the scale of payments alone. Their disenchantment was growing rapidly with other aspects of the Unemployent Act as it applied to Northern Ireland. It appeared to them that both stages were too heavily weighted in favour of the party in power.

The first stage which treated specifically those who had received transitional payments produced little change in the Outdoor Relief lists. The Opposition began to take a more critical view of the Government's position on the matter. Jack Beattie, who had earlier criticised the political appointments to the Assistance Board and Appeals Tribunals, raised on 24 March 1935 the judgement of the insurance umpire which rendered the insurance records of 3,500 applicants null and void. He acted on information that he had received privately from a memo sent out to the appeals tribunals from the Minister of Labour.[13]

This memo referred to terms which were contained in the 1920 Act setting up the state which enabled the Northern Ireland Insurance Umpire to interpret that Northern Ireland was not part of Great Britain but of the United Kingdom. This interpretation, quite incredibly, enabled insurance officers and appeals tribunals to disqualify insured contributors from receiving benefit while resident outside Great Britain, i.e. in the Free State, under the terms of the Unemployment Insurance Act 1935, Miscellaneous Disqualifications. Dealing with residence outside Great Britain it stated that disqualification would be imposed on claimants temporarily residing inside Northern Ireland. This interpretation also disqualified all persons living in the North who had been born in the Free State. It enabled the disqualification to be extended to voters' lists for local elections as well.

It was a perfect arrangement for the Government: once this interpretation was applied it could not be set aside except by parliamentary amendment. Yet because of the Government's absolute control of both legislative bodies, the Opposition, if they could find the resolve, would be blocked in any attempt they might make to change the interpretation in Parliament or in the Senate.

The implications of this interpretation were staggering in that decisions given by the Unemployment Insurance Appeal Tribunals were extended to determine the right of the people to vote in local elections. Westminster elections on the other hand were conducted on a different and fuller register and subject to different laws and hence were excluded from the consequences of this interpretation.

In any case the Umpire, whose rulings decided the precedents on which the entire insurance system was based, was rarely available. He was purportedly in ill-health and was allowed six months' holidays each year in the Bahamas while hundreds of insurance appeals built up. Beattie raised the question of his absence in the House so the Government was not unaware of it. Supplementary questions drew information from the Parliamentary Secretary of the Ministry of Labour that the insured population fell from 360,000 in 1924 to 344,000 in March 1936, and that 10,249 claims were disallowed by the Unemployment Assistance Tribunals during the period from February 1935 to February 1936.

Beattie complained further that private instructions from the Minister had been passed to chairmen of Appeals Tribunals that they alone and not the clerks should take written statements from claimants. This was a departure from a practice which the tribunal clerks had operated since 1912. It enabled chairmen, who were political appointees, to write reports in a way that kept benefit from 'undesirables' even if their cases warranted appeal. The whole procedure was a parody of the British Act on which it was allegedly based – the words of the Act were almost the same; the practice entirely different.

The Unionists used their powers with enormous shrewdness. They used all sorts of devices to discriminate against the Opposition. Since they had overwhelming control of government agencies and services, there was little difficulty in creating the machinery for appeals tribunals that suited them politically.

In reply to a parliamentary question from Midgley on 27 April 1937 on the number of people who applied for benefit under the 'Second Appointed Day' provisions, the Parliamentary Secretary said that 8,340 applied; 4,846 were accepted, 2,494 were disallowed and 1,000 were still under consideration. Only 1,071 came from the Belfast

Guardians' lists which at that time were still recording over 5,000 recipients.

The Parliamentary Secretary shed no light on what happened to the earlier number of 100,000 who were to be embraced under the second stage of the scheme according to the Minister of Labour when he introduced the Bill to Parliament on 29 May 1934.

It was made clear by the Minister of Labour when the Bill was first introduced in May 1934 that 100,000 people outside the scope of the unemployment insurance scheme would be eligible for unemployment assistance. Three years later a spokesman for the same Ministry admitted that only 5 per cent of the number eligible for benefit received it – in spite of the fact that the qualifications were met by the 95 per cent of those refused. The percentage of refusals was too great to admit of any interpretation other than that this was deliberate Government policy. Strategic requirements were more important than humane considerations!

Beattie by this time was already probing for information on the mystery. On 20 April 1937 he asked a further set of questions of the Minister of Labour, based on his experiences at the appeals tribunals which he visited each morning to assist constituents. The questions were intended to tease out legal definitions on what was meant by 'normally insurable employment' and 'not genuinely seeking employment'. Both qualifications were being used by the Government to prevent applicants other than their own supporters from receiving benefit. He asked the Minister of Labour:

1. if he could state the number of total stamps under the National Health Insurance and Widows, Orphans and Old Age Contribution Pensions Acts that an applicant must show to qualify for public assistance;

2. whether voluntary contributions stamps counted as qualification;

3. whether stamps received for relief work by the Belfast Board of Guardians would be accepted in calculation of total stamps required;

4. whether he was prepared to inform the House what 'normally insurable' meant in Northern Ireland, and

5. how it applied to Part 2 of the Unemployment Act 1934.

J.M. Andrews, Minister of Labour, replied to Beattie as follows:

The Act does not lay down any contribution test for determining whether an application for unemployment assistance is normally occupied in employment, insurable under the contributing Pensions Act. The question has to be decided in each particular case in relation to the individual's industrial record as a whole.

The duty of interpreting the conditions laid down by Parliament and of applying it to the widely differing types of cases which arise has been placed by statute on the officers of the Unemployment Assistance Board in the first instance and from their decision there is a right to appeal in each case to the chairman of the Tribunals.

Little wonder that Beattie in a supplementary question said that the reply was unsatisfactory: he had investigated the whole issue and had failed to find anywhere in Britain where the condition of an applicant being 'normally insurable' applied to the Insurance Act as it did to Part 2 of the Northern Ireland Act. He moved to have the section deleted but was heavily defeated in the subsequent vote. It was quite clear from the reply that the plan to administer unemployment assistance was being formulated by people who were politically acceptable to the Unionist Party, the direct opposite of what was intended by the Act in Britain. A month later, Midgley again attempted to have the section deleted but again suffered defeat.[14]

On 28 April 1937 Beattie returned to the subject of the estimates to claim that 100 people per week were being turned down because they were not insured under the Act in accordance with the Umpire's decisions that they were 'not genuinely seeking work' or were persons who had abandoned 'insurable' work. The numbers disqualified each week, if Beattie's figures were correct, were substantial enough to deter the unemployed from applying for assistance and to force other able-bodied unemployed to move to Britain in search of work. One thing certain, however, was that the skilled unemployed did not experience the same difficulty.

Later that year a new Poor Law Relief Act was introduced in Northern Ireland. It was confined to Northern Ireland and entailed some departures from the unemployment legislation.[15] It had been devised as a mopping-up operation to keep substantial numbers of the able-bodied unemployed from being absorbed into the unemployment assistance scheme.

It was a futile gesture in some ways because the Board of Guardians ignored it. They had no intention of continuing to pay relief to the able-bodied unemployed from rates when the Unemployment Act placed an obligation on the Government to do it. The Act had no relation to anything across the water where the Poor Law had been abolished. However, it was quite clear from the Minutes of the Guardians that it had been imposed on them at the instigation of the Party hierarchy who obviously had stressed in private the necessity of retaining it for party political purposes.

On 14 October 1937 Midgley, seeing through the Government's tactics of rendering the Act impotent, suggested that it was still not being made obligatory for Boards to pay relief to the able-bodied destitute. 'The Government,' he said, 'had violated its pledge to Britain that all legislation would proceed on parallel lines: in England the Poor Law was abolished and its functions transferred to local authorities with resources that could administer it better'. Midgley was supported by other MPs who by this time had accumulated ample evidence of the Government's duplicity.[16]

Beattie said that when the Minister of Labour introduced the Unemployment Bill he stated that those outside the scope of the Bill would be small in number, ie the pauper and vagrant class. But, the people at present affected were those who were at one time insured within the meaning of the Unemployment Insurance Act, had qualified for benefit but due to long-term unemployment had lost their qualification. They were now compelled to seek relief through the Poor Law. In Britain, those who had been out of employment for ten years and lost their insurability under the Unemployment Insurance Act were again being assisted. Under the Act, Umpires' decisions in Britain had established that unemployment of ten years did not remove entitlement to insurability.[17]

Beattie pursued the issue with tenacity. On 8 March 1938 he raised again on the Supplementary Estimates the decisions of the Umpire in Northern Ireland which were not keeping in step with those in Britain.

He quoted *Hansard* of 1937 which stated that on seven different decisions of the Umpire on insurability the Northern Irish law was different from that applying in England. He requested that the Northern Ireland position be abolished and that the English Umpire's decisions apply here.

Challenging the Government later on their reasons for not declaring Northern Ireland a Distressed Area, which it undoubtedly was because of its chronically high unemployment, and hence eligible

159

for Westminster grants towards economic development, Beattie said that they would have to pay 12s. 6d. per head for all those residing in the Distressed Area, whereas the Belfast Board of Guardians were only paying 4s. and other parts of the North were receiving even less. Unionist politicians when replying to Beattie's constant charges that Northern Ireland was a Distressed Area always denied this. They claimed that Northern Ireland had a healthy regional economy and that its people 'must take the rough with the smooth'. Unionists regarded allegations that they lived in an unsound regional economy in which a substantial number of people suffered from poverty and destitution as being treasonable. Unionist MPs who attended the Westminster Parliament voted consistently against all improvements to social security and never raised matters that reflected poorly on Northern Ireland. The efforts of the Free State Government to build their economy were treated with scorn. It was regarded as a propaganda war and Beattie's efforts to have Northern Ireland declared a Distressed Area to assist the poor were dismissed by Unionists for that reason.

On 25 October 1938, Paddy Agnew, a newly elected MP, took up Beattie's earlier theme when he moved to get the Government to bring the able-bodied unemployed under the same regulation for Outdoor Relief as in Britain. The main point in Agnew's speech was that the Government had selected only a portion of the British regulation for use in Northern Ireland, and had cast aside those provisions which compelled local government authorities to meet the needs of the able-bodied unemployed.

T. Henderson, MP, said in the same debate that the assistance boards were composed of persons with the same mentality as the members of the Government.

On 16 June 1939, after appointments were made to the Unemployment Assistance Board, the Opposition protested strongly to the Minister of Labour. Those appointed were, according to Beattie, either company directors or retired civil servants. The exception to the list was the wife of a serving civil servant – but all of them were emphatically linked to the Party.

The Guardians meanwhile were exceedingly unhappy with the way the Government was operating the 'Second Appointed Day'. From examining the Act itself as well as from letters which they received from the Prime Minister over the three years that it took the Bill to pass through Parliament, they were given to understand that their lists would be completely cleared of the able-bodied unemployed. The implementation of the Act did not measure up to their expectations. It had been reported in April 1938 that 1,750 cases from the Belfast list were assimilated into the scheme, leaving 850 still with the Board.[18] But the conditions for qualification that required applicants to have 200 stamps for the past ten years or 30 stamps over the last two years were imposed only in Northern Ireland. The Guardians were forced to carry the burden of 850 able-bodied unemployed on the Belfast rates.

The Guardians decided to seek a conference with the Ministry of Labour to point out that a large number of the able-bodied unemployed were still being relieved by them from Poor Law sources.

The deputation from the Board met the Unemployment Assistance Board on 21 May to discuss the number transferred from the Outdoor Relief lists under the 'Second Appointed Day' provisions. The Guardians pointed out correspondence which they had received from the Ministry of Labour stating that ordinary cases of relief would be the only ones that they would be required to consider. From their own records they recognised that some cases which had been turned down were more entitled to relief than many of those receiving benefit under the new arrangements.[19]

The Ministry replied to the delegation in writing. They pointed out that an Order – which the Guardians had the right to apply for – could be issued for a prescribed period which would enable them to make Poor Relief payments at their discretion subject to the recipient being a resident of the United Kingdom for seven years and registering for work at an Unemployment Exchange every fortnight.

The Ministry of Labour appeared to drag their feet on this complaint until the end of 1937. On 14 December, a letter was received from the Ministry informing the Guardians that they had considered their representations and were proposing to increase grants for road work schemes under the Belfast Corporation to 75 per cent.

By the winter of 1938 the Guardians came under attack from newspapers, politicians at Stormont, councillors at the City Hall, and from the general public, because of rumours of corruption and misconduct of their affairs. They had begun to quarrel amongst themselves over whether or not to seek a public inquiry into widespread allegations concerning the maladministration of their affairs.

The in-fighting at the Board which appeared unstoppable was relieved on one occasion by the arrival of a delegation from the

Unemployed Workers' Movement on 7 December 1938 to discuss the problems of hardship for those who had not received unemployment assistance benefit; ie single men and single women living with parents, single men in registered lodging houses and elderly people with no industrial record. The delegation claimed that grants were too small to provide them with clothing, enough food or coal in winter. They pointed out in addition that although the Board had power to appeal against decisions of the Unemployment Assistance Board, it had never done so.

The Board resolved, presumably feeling the need for a little public support, to pay an additional 5s. per week to all relief recipients during the months of November to March – it would be known henceforth as a special winter allowance.[20]

In January 1939, James Jamison, JP (Chairman of the Finance Committee), presenting the estimates for the year, stated that £29,885 was overspent on Outdoor Relief, due to a filtering back of cases from the Unemployment Assistance Board. He estimated that the rates would have to be increased by six pence in the pound and hoped that the Corporation would draw the able-bodied unemployed for their work schemes from the Guardians' lists. He believed it would lead to a reduction in Poor Law expenditure.

Figures for the first six months of 1939 on relief expenditure bore out what Jamison had said:

7 January 1939	3676 cases of Outdoor Relief received £2284. 3. 6.
4 February 1939	3898 cases of Outdoor Relief received £2338. 8. 6.
18 March 1939	4142 cases of Outdoor Relief received £2438. 3.10.
15 April 1939	4289 cases of Outdoor Relief received £1921.16. 6.
6 May 1939	4423 cases of Outdoor Relief received £1906.10. 6.
3 June 1939	4575 cases of Outdoor Relief received £1893. 5. 0.

The Guardians throughout this period were living on borrowed time because an inquiry had been held into their activities and the Cabinet had evidence submitted by the local Government Inspector to recommend their replacement.

On 9 March 1939 the Guardians were finally replaced by Commissioners. The announcement of this replacement was truly remarkable. Bates, speaking to Parliament on his ministerial estimates, suddenly informed members that the Guardians had been replaced by two Commissioners, one of whom had been in retirement and would receive an annual salary of £1,465 and the other who would supervise the Outdoor Relief Scheme and would receive a wage of £5 per week.

No further comment was made by Bates or by the Government side of the House in spite of efforts by the Opposition to get information. No other public announcement was ever made concerning the abolition of the Belfast Poor Law Guardians. Here was confirmation that the Poor Law structure and its role were important to the Unionist strategy. It was still to be kept alive to select applicants for relief on a political basis. The Commissioners were expected to continue to do the same work as the other Poor Law Boards were carrying out in rural areas.

With the outbreak of war in 1939 and the consequent reduction of the number of unemployed, a more hopeful existence for the able-bodied unemployed was brought about. This existence was helped too by a new piece of legislation which was brought in, hotfoot, to cope with the emergency.

The Unemployment Assistance (Emergency Powers) Act (Northern Ireland) 1939 extended powers to the Unemployment Assistance Board to meet whatever need arose from the wartime situation. By 1940 the Board received a new title, 'The Assistance Board', with the responsibility of supplementing the entire range of benefits set up by statute as well as those outside that framework. The new Act, for all practical purposes, ended the life of the Poor Law and ushered in the new era which in 1947 led to social benefits becoming the entitlement of every citizen in Northern Ireland.

11
The End of the Belfast Guardians

The life of the Belfast Board of Guardians was brought to an end in 1939, not as a consequence of its members' indifference to the sufferings of the Belfast poor nor of their refusal to support Unionist strategy but because the power they were given as Guardians corrupted them. Their use of this power from 1920 onwards brought them by degrees into public disrepute and they ended their administration squabbling over abuses that had by then become intolerable to their own party. They believed that they had been justified in all they had done. Had they not kept the rates down for years to the lowest level in the United Kingdom? Had they not denied relief to the work-shy who spent their time creating large families that they could not maintain? Had they not by these efforts saved the community from the 'enemies within the gates'? Yet, unlike Craig, Bates and Andrews, they never received the praise for their support of Party strategy.

Nonetheless they had long understood that the Government needed them more than they needed the Government. Bates, in his public office as Minister of Home Affairs and in his private office as Unionist Party Secretary, never quite succeeded in quelling them. They were conscious that Craig's and Bates' attitude to the distribution of relief justified theirs. Had they not witnessed on their visits to Unionist Party Headquarters in Glengall Street the flow of patronage dispensed by Craig and Bates to party supporters? Had they not an equal right to dispense patronage and indeed to receive it if by doing so they proved their loyalty to the Unionist cause?

They had long perceived that patronage at local government level was tolerated and encouraged by Craig and Bates in particular. They had witnessed Bates's attempt to cover up the blatant corruption in the Belfast Corporation concerning housing contracts.[1] Had Bates not claimed that an investigation would be damaging to the Party's interests?

Craig's handouts to local authorities and old cronies like Sir Samuel Kelly, which in some cases did not go through the parliamentary estimates, were part of the same ideology. This was what 'distributing bones for special purposes' was all about.

The Guardians had seen it as part of their jobs to keep the flow of patronage moving and if they as the Party 'faithful' received it also, so much the better. That was the aim of the exercise anyway. However, not every public representative or Guardian acquiesced in this behaviour. Excesses could and did bring objections from within the Party which loyalty to Party objectives could not entirely suppress. Nevertheless Party loyalty, in the face of political enemies in Belfast and in the Free State, had gradually retarded the application of moral standards to the conduct of public affairs. The process went too far and the day of reckoning arrived for the Guardians in 1939.

On 21 January 1933, in the wake of the Outdoor Relief riots, Beattie, in a parliamentary question, asked the Minister of Labour to investigate complaints that a levy was being imposed on the old age pensioners by the Master of the workhouse. The Minister replied, stating that he was having a Ministerial representative present each weekend at the workhouse to ensure that proper pensions were received by the inmates.

The reply caught Beattie by surprise. He did not expect that the Minister would respond so quickly to his question. It was clear that the Minister had received a report prior to the riots that the Master had been collecting the old age pension books of those receiving Indoor Relief and converting the money to his own use. This inquiry led, after a long delay, to the Master of the workhouse being prosecuted by the police. Over a period of 17 months £3,455 had been deducted from pensions. Each pension was for 10s. The Master allowed inmates 2s. each and lodged 8s. in a loan account from which he drew for his personal use. The Judge's remarks were critical of the affairs of the workhouse.

Beattie, speaking in a subsequent debate on the administration of the Belfast Union, said, 'it was illegal for the Union to deduct from old age pensions under the Old Age Pensons Act, yet the practice still continues'. He moved a motion for inquiry into workhouse administration. It was defeated by a vote of 19 to 5.

It was over two years before this case surfaced in the courts, although Beattie returned to it on 21 August 1934, according to the Parliamentary Reports. It merited little attention at the Guardians' meeting. The 'law of omerta' was just as effective amongst the Unionist Guardians as it was in the councils of the Sicilian Mafia. The only occasion that reference was recorded on this issue in the Minutes was when a solicitor was instructed to attend court to listen to the deposition being read out in the event of the Board's interest being affected. The Ministry of Home Affairs was responsible for the court lists as well as the police processing of criminal offences. No doubt Bates had tried his 'covering-up' tactics as well.

The Board's conduct was extraordinary because the allegation concerning the stealing of pensions was widespread. The *Irish News* on 4 March 1935 reported that the Master of the workhouse had been sentenced to six months' imprisonment for fraud. Scarcely a ripple came from the Board of Guardians on the losses sustained by the pensioners.

In December 1936 a special committee was set up to investigate two complaints made by Harry Diamond into the failure of two relieving officers (Districts 4 and 5) to pass on Christmas payments to recipients. The clerk reported that he had accompanied Mr Diamond to interview the families concerned. Both relieving officers were suspended and a sub-committee was set up to complete the investigations.

The sub-committee reported to the Board on 27 January 1937, to the effect that thirty-five payments were missed by the relieving officer for No. 4 District involving the sum of £25.1s.0d. and seven payments amounting to £1.6s.0d. by the relieving officer of No. 5 District. The Ministry was asked to remove them from office.

Diamond, like Beattie before him in Parliament, was surprised at the report he received from the Clerk of the Union. It seemed to represent a change of attitude by some members of the administration. In the past misdemeanours were concealed by everyone for the sake of Party loyalty. Indeed, the Ministry of Home Affairs Inspector, Vice-Admiral Archdale, in his annual report omitted to refer to the matter. His reports gave the impression that Poor Law affairs were in good order in spite of strong rumours in Belfast to the contrary.

The Board Minutes for 10 March 1937 show that a Unionist Guardian, C.M. Lowe, was recorded as asking too many questions about the behaviour of the Master of the workhouse; and the Ministry requested to exclude him from the workhouse. Archdale attended the next meeting and advised that Lowe was entitled to visit the workhouse but must subject himself to the normal code of conduct.

Lowe, according to the Minutes of the Board, made complaints about interference with patients' pensions on 6 April. He stated that some Guardians were getting the Master drunk and taking anything they wanted out of the workhouse while he was in that state. Collins seized on the opportunity to move that the Ministry be requested to establish an inquiry into Lowe's allegations. Lowe immediately refused to discuss them and no further reference to them was made in the Minutes.

Lowe's reason for dropping his allegations may be that he was subject to party censure for raising such a divisive issue. Opposition members, like Collins, were never allowed to exploit differences within the Unionist Party. It was fear of Party censure on matters like these that caused public representatives of the Unionist Party to close ranks and avoid references in public to the Guardians' misdemeanours.

On 2 March 1938 Archdale submitted his annual report on the Guardians' activities to the Ministry. It was markedly different from the usual submissions. He said that the present system overlapped, created hardship and differential treatment of cases; under present procedures one responsible official could carry out the duties with saving in staff and increased efficiency. The Guardians were asked to comment.[2]

There is a strong possibility that Archdale's letter was intended to detonate the combustible material which in recent months lay concealed below the surface of the Guardians' activities. Allegations of impropriety against them and Board officials laced every report and minute written at the time. The further possibility existed that the Government had transferred a substantial amount of relief to their political appointees in the assistance boards and were therefore in a position to rid themselves of the scourge that the Belfast Guardians had become. The Government had now created the conditions for getting rid of them; they could now abolish them without the need to revoke the legislation which covered the Boards outside Belfast. This move would keep the overall strategy intact.

The bombshell which was to blow them apart was exploded on 13 April 1938 by James B. Butler, local government auditor, who wrote an extraordinary interim report on the audit of the Belfast Poor Law administration for 1937.[3]

Butler, referring to his reports of previous years, described the workhouse stores' records as unsatisfactory and decided for himself to make a closer examination of the procedures for stocktaking. He found that bulk stores were not counted. Figures were pencilled in and inked over by the Master of workhouse and were similar in quantities to those of the previous year. The master, when challenged by Butler, admitted that he had supplied them to the stocktaker.

The auditor stated that 'it was a very serious stage of affairs. There was no check whatever on stores or on those responsible for counting them. It was impossible', he claimed, 'to ascertain loss of stock because of collusion between master and stocktaker'. He continued:

> Under Article 42, Section 2, of the Union Accounts Order 1905, the Master is expressly forbidden to allow the stocktaker to have access to any books or records of the Workhouse for the purpose of stock-taking. The Master's action was in direct defiance of that section of the order.

The matter of a public inquiry into the affairs of the Union had been raised on several occasions in the past by members but nothing had ever come of it. However, a meeting of the Board which was convened to consider the auditor's report passed a resolution by eighteen votes to six, asking the Ministry to hold a sworn inquiry into the matters raised in the report.

On 28 June 1938, R. Clements Lyttle, JP, a Guardian who represented the area in which the workhouse was located, moved that the Government hold a broad sworn inquiry into the entire Poor Law operations and alleged in his speech that a number of Guardians were trying to cover up for certain officials who were in contact with Party officers in the Unionist Headquarters.

Lyttle was referring to Edmund Warnock, KC, who was Parliamentary Secretary to the Minister of Home Affairs, and by this time in virtual charge of the Ministry, as Bates was beginning to bow under the pressure of his age. Warnock represented the area in Parliament where the workhouse was located. Many of those affected by the inquiry were his strongest supporters and election workers. It was not in his interest to let this matter get out of hand. He succeeded in turning the matter back on to Lyttle and after a bitter row in the local Party, Lyttle was charged with disloyalty to the Government and forced to resign from the Party.

The Ministry of Home Affairs replied to the Guardians' letter of 19 July, stating that they would be glad to meet representatives of the Board to discuss these matters.[4]

A concerted effort was made by a group of Unionist Guardians to have a resolution passed stating that the system of stocktaking was inefficient, out of date, and that the officials who were criticised by the auditor were not really to blame.

Mr William Cochrane, JP, who tried physically to prevent the earlier meeting coming to a conclusion, gave notice of a rescinding motion:

> that the Clerk of the Union and the Master of the workhouse together bring in a full and comprehensive report on stock and embody with the report suggestions for better administration of the workhouse.

Another letter dated 29 July was received from the Ministry in which unease was expressed concerning the attitude of the Guardians at their meeting on 19 July and which asked them to set up a committee of inquiry to investigate the implications of the auditor's report. The meetings became a 'Tower of Babel'.

As a result of the public infighting between the Guardians who supported a sworn inquiry and those who did not, a further report was sent to the Ministry of Home Affairs by the Government auditor, H.D. Strain; a copy which went to the Guardians referred again to abuse of the financial procedures that arose out of the local government auditor's report.[5]

The auditor, who was bent on having action taken on this occasion, pointed out that £145 had been spent on the removal of rubbish from the workhouse while the workhouse lorry was available. Moreover, he informed the Ministry that he had struck out four payments for this removal under Section 12 of the Local Government (Ireland) Act 1871, and surcharged £7.10.0. against the person who issued the authority for the payments to be made.

In addition, he asked for the following items to be reconsidered:

1. Revision of tender forms to suit current requirements.
2. Detention of all samples submitted by tender, especially where one other than the lowest has been accepted.
3. Adjusting of transfers of money between Master's and old age pensioners' bank account, the special Bank Deposit Account and the General Revenue Account.
4. The present system of cash collection and stores accounting, the former including control of the Old Age Pension Bank Account which was not shown in the ledger but has a credit balance of £1,097.6.3. at December 1937.

The matter dragged on without resolution into the autumn and on

4 October Mrs F.E. Breakie, a Unionist Guardian, moved that all Board members be appointed to the committee set up to investigate the auditor's report. The ensuing discussion brought out the fact that the Committee's work was being obstructed again by certain Guardians preventing proper questions being asked of Poor Law officials.

A number of Guardians led by Clements Lyttle decided to write to the Prime Minister concerning the harm being done by the recalcitrant Guardians. They asked Craig privately to hold an inquiry into the Guardians' conduct of affairs. By this time the tide of public opinion was running so strongly against the Guardians that Sir Crawford McCullagh, Lord Mayor of Belfast, snubbed them when they came to the City Hall to lay a wreath at the Cenotaph on Armistice Day. He asked them to withdraw without laying the wreath. The incident was reported with bitterness in the Board's Minutes later that month. Meanwhile Craig brought the matter of the Guardians' conduct to the attention of the Cabinet and Warnock was requested to attend specially to answer allegations based on comments he was purported to have made at recent private meetings of St Anne's constituency party.

On 10 October, after the Cabinet had deliberated on the matter, the Minister of Home Affairs issued a public statement agreeing to hold an inquiry into the operation of the Poor Law in Belfast. John Dunlop was appointed chairman, with Vice-Admiral Archdale to assist in the investigation. Dunlop was the specialist on Home Affairs inquiries, well known for imposing high standards of public duty on Poor Law representatives throughout the country. He was appointed by Bates several years later to the position of Town Clerk of Belfast when excesses there were getting out of hand.

Dunlop's inquiry, set up on 7 November 1938, was conducted in private and acted as a signal to the Guardians to step up their in-fighting. The Clerk, who was legally bound to assist with providing information for the inquiry, was the subject of vicious and persistent attacks from certain members at each meeting. He dutifully recorded these in the Board's records.

On 9 March the Board was informed that the Master of the work-house had been directed by the Minister of Home Affairs to tender his resignation. On 15 March the Minister of Home Affairs issued an Order Under Seal, beginning:

Whereas through the default of the Board of Guardians of the Belfast Union the duties of the said Board have not been duly and effectively discharged according to the intention of the said several Acts in force for relief of the destitute poor in Northern Ireland.

The report went on to refer to the appointment of two Commissioners to replace the Board, namely Mr Henry Diamond, OBE, M.A., and Mr Llywellyn Drysdale Innis Graham, M.B., B.Ch.[6]

In the course of his speech in Parliament Bates estimated that the appointment of Commissioners would save the ratepayers of Belfast £35,000 annually. Already he noted that 1,000 tons of coal amounting to £1,500 had been saved and that the former Guardians were being surcharged for over-ordering 546 yards of corduroy.

The appointment of the Commissioners became the cause of amusement for Tommy Henderson the following day at Stormont. Speaking on the vote for the supply account for Home Affairs, he got the Minister to admit that the administration of the workhouse 'had always stunk in his nostrils'. The significance of the speech was that it made no reference whatever to the administration of the Outdoor Relief. In the case of the workhouse it would have been a simple exercise to transfer it directly to a department of the Belfast Corporation for administration.[7]

The inquiry had been held and the report lodged with the Prime Minister at Stormont Castle for a number of months before he was pressed into taking action on it. Dunlop was particularly angry as he had found and reported solid evidence of widespread corruption amongst officials and Guardians. In spite of his efforts to have the report published, it was decided not to publish it but to accept only the recommendations made by Dunlop.

The *Belfast Telegraph*, a leading Unionist paper, had carried an editorial on the Guardians when it appeared that no action was to be taken on the report. It said that:

We deplore the pass to which affairs have come in the public life of Belfast that the Government should be under the painful necessity of removing administration from the hands of one of our Boards... there is no disguising that it is a blot... for what we stand for... the fault lies not with the Government but with those members of the Guardians whose derelictions have led to the present denouncement.[8]

On 20 March in Parliament, Tommy Henderson asked for a copy of the Warnock speech to Orangemen in Sandy Row Orange Hall where he had allegedly promised retaliation against those responsible for forcing the inquiry. Warnock was accused by Henderson of having discussed the inquiry at an Orange Order meeting but not in Parliament.

J.W. Nixon wanted to know why the report was not to be published.

> It was the practice always to make public reports of public inquiries in the same way that the inquiry into the affairs of the Pig Marketing Board had been made public a short time before the debate.

Henderson kept pressure on Warnock because of his close connection with the scandal. After referring to the former workhouse master receiving six months' imprisonment for fraud, he forced Warnock to admit to further discrepancies which were never made public. On 28 March 1939, Warnock stated that in 1935–6 the local government auditor drew attention to the unsatisfactory nature of the accounts of the Board of Guardians. In 1937 the auditor reported adversely on the system of store accounts and in 1938 he again emphasised that the same problems were present in the accounts and book-keeping and insisted on the Board of Guardians taking action to revise the stock-taking system.[10] But Archdale's reports on the work of the Guardians during these same years were always couched in approving terms.

Warnock was stating in public for the first time the real depth of the Guardians' abuse of their public responsibilities. He was implicitly condemning at the same time the more important abuse of public office on the part of the Government by acquiescing in these malpractices – the auditor's reports were unassailable evidence of constant corruption. Bates, who was the Minister responsible for the Guardians' conduct, as usual did nothing about them because the Party strategy was at stake.

Bates was the pivotal figure in making that strategy work. His ministerial functions, his accessibility to Party members, his ability to manipulate men from the Prime Minister down to his office boy, involved him in the monitoring of the strategic mechanism, making certain that it was oiled by the free flow of patronage from his office. He recognised that loyalty to the Party deserved reward: but this concept of Government strategy was taken a step further by the Poor

Law Guardians of Belfast: with disastrous results. If it was not wrong to give cash relief to a Party supporter, it could not be wrong to give an odd ton of coal or box of groceries to a Party Guardian. The dangers inherent in this concept finally became too great to be borne. It was this wide and naked malpractice and the fear of the damage it could do to the Party that compelled three Guardians to write to Craig begging him to have it stopped. Senior members of the Party rather than members of the Government made the arrangements to end the Belfast Board of Guardians, while leaving the other Boards in the North still operating. The other Boards were still integral to the Unionist strategy of maintaining control of its opposition.

Craig, by this time an old man, was unable to concentrate his mind on such a problem. He barely attended his office and all work was brought to his living quarters at Stormont Castle. Dunlop's report lay on his desk until pressure from within the Party forced him to take action on the Guardians' proven misconducts.

The Belfast ratepayers' tolerance of the Guardians misdemeanours had at last worn out. The earlier immunity, extended to them because of their close links – both geographical and political – with Unionist Headquarters in Glengall Street, by now had been withdrawn. In their final days their bickerings became more ridiculous and resulted in adverse publicity for the Party. It was not for these reasons alone that its life as a Poor Law Board came to an end. It came about when the welter of corruption attached to its activities became so odious that it threatened the overall strategy of the Government, especially in other Poor Law areas where it had to function effectively as a social control instrument. But it had to go and it did go – to the mocking sounds of Tommy Henderson's laughter!

12
Conclusions

I have examined four themes in this book:

1. the discriminatory treatment and containment of Catholics and non-Unionists from the disorders of the middle of the nineteenth century to the more systematic pressures exerted by the Unionist Government after its establishment in 1920;
2. the separation of workers on a sectarian basis, the skilled Protestants from the unskilled Catholics, which enabled the bourgeoisie to exploit the separation for economic and political reasons;
3. the continuous Unionist policy of focusing political activity on traditional sectarian issues in order to stifle the growth of an effective labour opposition in Ulster;
4. the alienation of substantial parts of the Belfast working classes by the excesses of their Board of Guardians, leading to its ultimate abolition.

Violence

In the first half of the nineteenth century Catholics arrived in Belfast in such numbers that the earlier settlers feared that they would lose their jobs, their houses, their religious freedom and their social standing. Their fears exploded into religious rioting against the newcomers (who had been welcomed at first by local entrepreneurs who needed their labour to help produce ships and linen for developing world markets).

In the 1860s the riots against Catholics coincided with the growth of the Orange Order and the fall in world trade. The effects of the riots caused a noticeable reduction in the Catholic population of Belfast and riots continued regularly until 1920 when the Northern Ireland state was established. But the continuing presence of Catholics in considerable numbers was looked upon as a danger to the new Government which saw one of its tasks as defending the Protestant faith against the threat of Catholicism.

Social and economic deprivation

The social policy of the Government of Northern Ireland after its establishment in 1920 was directed towards forcing Catholics and labour supporters by economic deprivation to emigrate or to limit their families. At the same time, their rioting mobs of supporters were driving Catholics back into ghetto areas where their votes would be rendered harmless.

This policy had to be comprehensively applied to be successful. It was necessary for it to extend into job and relief deprivation as well as electoral inequality.

During the first four years of its life the Unionist Government cared little about the consequences of their hard-line policies towards Catholics, but they were brought up with a severe jolt when Stephen Tallents, a civil servant sent to Ireland by the Colonial Office to investigate the general situation there, reported back to Westminster late in 1922 on their refusal to employ Catholics on relief work: as a result they were compelled to introduce a ratio of one Catholic to every two Protestants in each subsequent scheme. The realisation that Westminster would intervene on matters associated with this issue brought a degree of caution into administrative affairs but not into the affairs of the Belfast Poor Law Guardians.

The Unionists' failure to follow the lead of Britain and the Free State in the abolition of the Guardians can be explained only on the grounds that they wished to retain the principle of discretion in their administration of relief to the needy. What cannot be explained however is the failure of the Northern Ireland Government to keep social security expenditure in line with Britain. From 1926 to 1934 unemployment insurance expenditure in Britain increased by ten times the amount spent in 1926 but in Northern Ireland it increased by a mere 50 per cent.

From 1931 onwards legislation was introduced in Britain which ought to have been translated in its entirety to Northern Ireland under the parity arrangements of 1925. Such legislation on social security, including the Poor Law, was amended to remove automatic entitlement to benefit and to maintain the measure of discretion that the Unionists needed to preserve pressure on the Catholic minority.

On 1 January 1935, the 'First Appointed Day' of the Unemployment Act was reached in Northern Ireland. Its application was confined to those who worked in the general engineering industries, usually Government supporters, and administered in such a way that it assisted them exclusively.

It was stated explicitly by the Ministry of Labour on a number of occasions that a further 100,000 would be embraced within two months. But the 'Second Appointed Day' was delayed for two years and less than 5,000 were brought into the second stage of the scheme.

By this time political appointments had been made to the Tribunals and Appeals structures. Hundreds of Catholic families were denied benefit as the political appointees applied the device of disqualification. It was declared that they were either 'not genuinely seeking work' or, more disingenuously 'not normally in insurable employment'.

Moreover, the Government's refusal to have Northern Ireland declared a Distressed Area which would have entitled its able-bodied poor to extra grants from Westminster came at a time when as a region it was the most distressed in Britain. It bears out the proposition that the policy was devised to deprive Catholics of state aid to which they were entitled.

Conflict with Labour

The third theme of this book is demonstrated by the indifference of the bourgeoisie to the pogrom mounted against Catholics in July 1920. This indifference, deliberately contrived, was not only to hide their part in the pogrom but to rid themselves of the shop-stewards' movement that would have co-ordinated resistance to wage cuts which were envisaged: indeed, which reduced the wages of engineering workers by half over a period of five years.

Big business, the other side of the Unionist coin, had become alarmed by the militancy demonstrated by Belfast workers in 1919 – a militancy which hardened with the return of soldiers seeking employment at the end of the war. With the Unemployment Insurance Fund in deficit, the able-bodied unemployed of Northern Ireland received less in relief than their brothers elsewhere in Britain.

The Government's collusion with employers on this matter was never concealed. They sided unashamedly with Belfast's industrial barons and never tried to hide the fact. The policy was compounded by Carson in July 1920, when he encouraged the Orange wreckers to attack their shop stewards under the pretext that they were the 'Trojan horse of the IRA'.

To contain the Catholic section of the population within manageable proportions it was necessary for the Unionist Government to devise a method that would not draw the unwelcome attention of Westminster.

Since the riots had concentrated the Catholics into ghettoes and their elected representatives refused to attend Parliament, the Unionists set about a systematic withholding of relief that was calculated to be a more decisive deterrent to Catholics than the pre-1920 riots. But they had to operate by stealth.

The Unionist Government encouraged the Board of Guardians to develop their own brand of discretion towards those whom they had to relieve. They identified by use of the domestic means test those who were to be relieved and those who were not. The number of those helped by the Poor Law Guardians in the early years of Unionist rule was exceedingly small in comparison to those relieved by the St Vincent de Paul Society. This organisation, which exclusively helped Catholic poor, was for a time helping eight people for every one helped by the Poor Law Guardians in Belfast.

The Government tended to rely on the natural prejudices of the Guardians to deprive Catholics of relief and hence to secure their strategic objectives. They had *not* counted on the Guardians' prejudices being applied to the poor in every section of Belfast society, or on their stringent application causing the Protestant working class to join with Catholics in large-scale rioting against the Government in 1932. This development caused the Government, independently and against the wishes of the Guardians, to improve the scale of relief. In doing so they deliberately accentuated the element of discretion involved in granting relief to the needy, bringing both sections of the working class into violent conflict.

This policy had always determined the Unionists' attitude to the labour movement. It was confirmed by Craig in 1929 when he moved to abolish the system of Proportional Representation. He reiterated Carson's argument that 'the existence of Labour politicians in Parliament represented a danger to the State's security'. Consequently, Labour candidates in subsequent elections were subject to extreme abuse and physical attack.

The Belfast Poor Law Guardians
The fourth theme of this study is the excessive behaviour of the Guardians, not only towards the Catholic poor, but to the Protestant poor as well.

Basically, the Guardians understood their role as one of providing relief to the Belfast destitute. Their records and minutes of the early Twenties, however, indicate the restrictive nature of their application of the Poor Law and their disregard of their obligation to relieve the destitute outside the workhouse.

These Guardians were drawn mainly from the shopkeeper class and elected constantly from the narrow confines of the Belfast business community. They felt that they were doing a public service by keeping the rates down and being in the front line of the movement to force malingerers to work and away from the Relief Agency. Their complacency grew in the late Twenties when they forced the Northern Ireland Government to accept a labour test for able-bodied unemployed, something which no other Board in England could achieve. Local opinion, as expressed in Unionist Headquarters, was that they had carried out a public service. This praise went quickly to their heads and they came to believe that they were the 'public conscience' on matters affecting the poor.

By degrees, they acquired the arrogance as well as the power of the absolute ruler. They realised that their decisions determined whether families remained in the North or left it. Ultimately, in some extreme cases, they even had the power of life and death over certain destitute families by granting or denying relief.

This arrogance so blinded them that they unwittingly drew both sections of the working class together against them. After the Government intervened to force them to give extra financial help to the destitute, they still refused to listen. Personal feuding and corruption finally brought the Board to an end.

They had refused to recognise that they were merely an instrument of administrative control, exercising discretion in a politically selected way against the Government's opposition. The power which was handed to them by their Party destroyed them and nearly destroyed the Party on whose behalf they used it.

These four themes may be inter-related through the following analysis. In its early years, the Unionist administration maintained its hegemony through a combination of physical violence and the procedures available under the unemployment insurance legislation and the Poor Law provisions. When the violence became too much for the British Government to stomach, there was increasing reliance on the socialised violence provided by the discretionary powers of the Poor Law Guardians.

Unfortunately for the Unionist Government, the Guardians, because of their class background, vigorously applied their powers against both Catholic and Protestant unemployed. This resulted in the temporary unity of the poor on the basis of common misery. It was a unity which the Unionist Government feared might become permanent.

Thus, the eventual dissolution of the Board could not be interpreted as a humanitarian or progressive gesture on the part of Unionism. It was abandoned because it threatened the immediate goal of the hierarchy – the division of Protestant and Catholic working classes – and ultimately their strategy of retaining control of the state apparatus.

Appendix
Poor Law Legislation

The Poor Law Relief Act of 1838 provided for relief only in the workhouse. Views were expressed in Parliament prior to the passing of this Act that relief outside the workhouse should be prohibited because it would be dangerous to the general interests of the community.

Poor Law Relief Extension Act, 1847
The famine of 1846–7 placed an unbearable strain on the Poor Law administration causing Parliament to relax its application of the 1838 Act. In 1847 the Poor Law Relief Extension Act was introduced enabling relief to be given outside the workhouse for a temporary period. This Act authorised Guardians to grant relief either indoor or outdoor:

Section 1 – At all times, at their discretion, to destitute poor persons either *permanently* disabled from labour by age or infirmity, etc., or *temporarily* disabled by sickness or accident, and to destitute widows having two or more legitimate children dependent upon them.

Section 2 – Under special circumstances and for limited periods to such other classes as might be designated by Orders to be temporarily issued from time to time by the central authority. The special powers conferred by this latter section could, however, only be exercised by the central authority in the event of the workhouse being full or rendered unfit for occupation by the prevalence of infectious diseases, etc.

Section 7 – The relieving officer was authorised to afford between the meetings of the Boards of Guardians 'provisional relief', in any of the forms therein described, to any destitute person, to whatever class belonging, in all cases 'of sudden and urgent necessity'.

Section 10 – laid down that no person in occupation of more than a quarter of an acre of land could be deemed to be destitute, and that it was not therefore lawful for the Guardians to relieve such person either in or out of the workhouse.

Section 11 – required that an Outdoor Relief register be kept and submitted to the Guardians at each meeting.

Local Government (Ireland) Act, 1898

Section 13 of this Act provided the legislation that enabled relief to be granted for periods because of exceptional circumstances.

Section 13

(1) Where the Guardians of any Union satisfy the Council of a County that exceptional distress exists in some district electoral division situate both in the Union and in the County, and the Council apply to the Local Government Board, the Board may, if they think fit, by Order authorise the Guardians, subject to the prescribed conditions, to administer relief out of the workhouse for, say, time not exceeding two months from the date of the Order to poor persons of any description resident in the said electoral division, and may revoke any such Order either wholly or partly or with reference to any particular class of person.

(2) Section 2 of the Poor Law Relief (Ireland) Act 1862 (which excludes an occupier of more than a quarter of an acre from being relieved otherwise than in the workhouse), shall not apply as regards relief given under this Section (a).

(3) One half of any expenditure incurred in pursuance of an Order under this section shall be levied off the County at large (so, however, that the total amount of such expenditure levied off the County at large in any one year shall not exceed a sum equal to threepence in the pound on the rateable value of the County), and the Council of the County may nominate one of their members who shall be an additional member of the Board of Guardians for the period fixed by the Order.

(4) The Guardians may, with the consent of the Local Government Board, obtain for the purpose of this section temporary advances of such amount and for such period and repayable in such a manner as that Board may sanction, and may mortgage their property and funds to secure such advances.

Poor Law Relief (Amendment) Act (Northern Ireland), 1937

Section 13 of the Local Government (Ireland) Act 1898 had been repealed by the Poor Law Relief (Exceptional Distress) Act (Northern Ireland) 1928 which in turn was replaced by the Poor Law Relief (Amendment) Act (Northern Ireland) 1937. It was under the latter Act that Outdoor Relief to able-bodied unemployed was finally administered in Northern Ireland.

Section 1 of this Act states:

1. A Board of Guardians may, at their discretion, grant Outdoor Relief under Section 1 of the Poor Law Relief (Ireland) Act 1847 to any able-bodied destitute person who:–
   (a) has been resident in the United Kingdom for a continuous period of seven years prior to the date of his application for relief;
   (b) registers fortnightly in pursuance of the Labour Exchange Act 1909 for employment at an employment exchange within the meaning of the Unemployment Insurance Act (Northern Ireland) 1937, and
   (c) is unable to support himself or any persons ordinarily and actually dependent upon him.

Under this Section a sealed Order from the Ministry was no longer necessary; sub-section (c) allowed relief to single persons.

Under Section 13 of the Local Government (Ireland) Act 1898 the Corporation refunded to the Guardians half the costs of relief awarded under this Section. Under the 1928 Act the Corporation bore all the cost; but under the 1937 Act the Guardians were responsible for the full cost.

Relief awarded under the 1937 Act was no longer considered to be exceptional distress relief. There was provision made under this Act to enable the Ministry of Home Affairs, if satisfied either on representations made to it by the Board of Guardians of the Union or otherwise, to authorise by Order the Board of Guardians to grant Outdoor Relief during any prescribed period to poor persons resident in the said Union who would be excluded from receiving Outdoor Relief by the operation of Section 2 of the Poor Law Relief (Ireland) Act 1862.

The foregoing Section was amended by the 1937 Act so that the relevant part of the quarter acre clause, as later amended by sub-section 2 of Section 36 of the Local Government Act 1934, read 'land of a net annual value greater than four pounds', instead of 'land of a net annual value greater than three pounds'.

Unemployment Assistance (Emergency Powers) Act (Northern Ireland) 1939

This Act was introduced to obtain powers to extend the Unemployment Assistance Board activities to meet whatever need arose from the exigencies of the war-time situation.

By 1940 the Board had received a new title, 'The Assistance Board', with the responsibility of supplementing the entire range of benefits set up by statute as well as those outside the statutory framework. The new title and the additional responsibility sounded the death knell of the infamous 'means test'. It was from these modest and primitive Acts that the advance towards comprehensive social security began.

Relief in Cash or Kind

Guardians had discretionary powers to give relief either in cash or in kind. They refused to give it in cash for they suspected that recipients would use the money to gamble or buy intoxicants to the detriment of the family. To give relief in kind had two disadvantages – there was no provision made for the payment of rent; and, often, less groceries were received than were specified on the chit. Relief in kind caused widespread abuse, mainly by the grocer, and should have been stopped much earlier than it was.

Definition of Destitution

The Poor Law Acts relating to Outdoor Relief had always laid down that to be eligible for relief the applicant must be destitute. In the final report of the Royal Commission on Unemployment Insurance, November 1932, an effort is made to clarify the term 'destitution'. Section 103 states, *inter alia*, 'the qualification for relief under the Poor Law has always been what is called "destitution", namely the absence of the necessary means to maintain the applicant for relief and his dependants.' The term 'destitution' had no statutory definition. It was, however, defined by the Legal Adviser of the Local Government Board in his evidence before the Royal Commission of 1909 in the following terms:

'Destitution' when used to describe the condition of a person as a subject for relief implies that he is for the time being without material resources:

1. directly available;
2. appropriate for satisfying his physical needs...

183

(a) whether actually existing, or

(b) likely to arise immediately.

By 'physical needs' in this definition are meant such needs as must be satisfied:

1. in order to maintain life;
   or
2. in order to obviate, mitigate or remove causes endangering or likely to endanger life or impair health or bodily fitness for self-support.

This definition was testated in a circular issued by the Local Government Board in 1910, in which the Boards of Guardians were reminded that in determining whether an applicant for relief was or was not destitute –

they have to remember that a person may be destitute in respect of the want of some particular necessity of life without being destitute in the sense that he is entirely devoid of the means of subsistence; he may yet be destitute in that he is unable to provide for himself the particular form of medical attendance or treatment of which he is in urgent need.

References

Chapter I: Unionist Strategy and Structures

1. Anders Boserup, *Contradictions and Struggles in Northern Ireland,* (London, 1972), pp.157–92.
2. Geoffrey Bell, *Protestants of Ulster* (London, 1976), p.86.
3. Michael Farrell, *The Orange State* (London, 1976), p.27.
4. Patrick Buckland, *The Factory of Grievances* (Dublin, 1979), p.14.
5. Paul Bew, Peter Gibbon and Henry Patterson, *The State in Northern Ireland 1921–1972* (Manchester, 1979), p.76.
6. *Ibid.,* p.79.
7. Buckland, *op. cit.,* p.150.
8. *Ibid.,* p.151.
9. *Ibid.,* p.152.
10. *Ibid.,* p.152.
11. *Ibid.,* p.154.
12. John Whyte, 'Intra-Unionist Dispute', in *Economic and Social Review,* 1973, p.99.
13. R.J. Lawrence, *The Government of Northern Ireland 1921–64* (London, 1965), Appendix 3, p.192.

Chapter 2: Earlier Struggles of Catholics in Belfast

1. Emyrs Jones, 'The distribution and segregation of Roman Catholics in Belfast', *Sociological Review,* New Series IV, 1956.
2. *Ibid.*
3. R.H. Tawney, introduction to Max Weber, *The Protestant Ethic and the Spirit of Capitalism* (London, 1930).
4. Belinda Probert, *Beyond Orange and Green* (London, 1978) p.63.
5. Francis Piven and Richard Cloward, *Regulating The Poor* (London, 1972), p.224.
6. Sybil E. Baker, 'Orange and Green', in H.J. Dyos and M. Wolff (eds.), *The Victorian City* (London, 1973), vol. 2, p.801.
7. *Ibid.*
8. Jones, *op. cit.*
9. Rev. William O'Hanlon, *Walks Amongst the Poor of Belfast* (Belfast, 1953).
10. Cathal O'Byrne, *As I Roved Out* (Dublin, 1946), p.222.

11. G.B. Kenna, 'Facts and Figures of the Belfast Pogrom 1920–1922' (unpublished; copy in Linen Hall Library, Belfast).
12. Ian Budge and Cornelius O'Leary, *Belfast: Approach to Crisis 1613–1970* (London, 1973).
13. Kenna, *op. cit.*

Chapter 3: Early Trade Unions in Belfast

1. Sybil E. Baker, 'Orange and Green', in H.J. Dyos and M. Wolff (eds.), *The Victorian City* (London, 1973).
2. *Ibid.*
3. E.J. Hobsbawn, *Labouring Men* (London, 1964), p.302.
4. William McMullen, unpublished memoirs. McMullen was a full-time official, later General President, of the Irish Transport and General Workers' Union; member of Parliament (Northern Ireland) 1925–9; Poor Law Commissioner in Belfast 1924–5; member of Senate 1951–4. It is the intention of the ITGWU to have McMullen's memoirs published.
5. *Ibid.*
6. Anthony J. Gaughan, *Tom Johnson* (Dublin, 1980) p.24.
7. John Boyle, lecture on the Belfast Trades Council, 1890–1914, given in Dublin, September 1980.
8. McMullen, *op. cit.*
9. *Ibid.*
10. John Boyle, *Leaders and Workers: Thomas Davis Lectures* (Dublin, 1961), p.60.

Chapter 4: The Setting-up of the Northern Ireland Regime

1. Lord Longford, *Peace by Ordeal* (London, 1935) p.69.
2. *House of Common Debates*, 5th series, vol. 26, col. 1458.
3. John F. Harbinson, *The Ulster Unionist Party 1882–1973* (Belfast, 1973), p.166.
4. G.B. McKenna, 'Facts and Figures of the Belfast Pogrom, 1920–1922', (unpublished; copy in the Linen Hall Library, Belfast).
5. Patrick Buckland, *The Factory of Grievance* (Dublin, 1979), p.22.
6. Paul Bew, Peter Gibbon and Henry Patterson, *The State in Northern Ireland 1921–72* (Manchester, 1979), p.77.
7. Dame Enid Lyons, *So We Take Comfort* (London, 1965).
8. Bew *et al, op. cit.*, p.81.
9. Denis Barrett and Charles Carter, *A Study in Group Relations* (Oxford, 1962), p.86.
10. St John Ervine, *Craigavon, Ulsterman* (London, 1949), p.516.
11. Geoffrey Bell, *Protestants of Ulster* (London, 1976), p.86.
12. Michael Farrell, *The Orange State* (London, 1976), p.27.
13. Robert Chesshyre, article on Iain Maclean, *Observer* magazine, 13 July 1970.
14. Maclean, *Popular Protest and Public Order* (London, 1974), p.222.
15. Tom Jones, *Whitehall Diary* (London, 1969), vol. 1, p.99.
16. Bew *et al, op. cit.*, p.48.

17. Kenna, *op. cit.*
18. Andro Linklater, *Unhusband Life* (London, 1970), p.222.
19. J.D. Clarkson, *Labour and Nationalism in Ireland* (New York, 1925), p.365.
20. *Ibid.*, p.370.
21. Trades Union Conference report, 1921, pp.267–77.
22. *Ibid.*
23. L. O'Nullain, *Finances of Partition* (Dublin, 1952), p.31.
24. Clarkson, *op. cit.,* p.384.
25. *Ibid.*
26. John A. Oliver, *Working at Stormont* (Dublin, 1978), p.38.
27. *The Labour Opposition,* January 1926 (copy in Linen Hall Library, Belfast).

Chapter 5: The Poor Law in Ireland

1. R.B. McDowell, *The Irish Administration, 1801–1914* (London, 1964), p.179.
2. Sir John Newport, *Select Committee Report on the Labouring Poor in Ireland,* 1819.
3. F.S.L. Lyons, *Ireland since the Famine* (London, 1971), p.35.
4. James S. Donnelly, *Land and People of Nineteenth Century Cork* (London, 1975), p.18.
5. Sir George Nicholls, Poor Law in Ireland Government Reports, 1849.
6. *Ibid.*
7. Lyons, *op. cit.,* p.79.
8. Cathal O'Byrne, *As I Roved Out* (Belfast, 1939) p.218.
9. Maurice Bruce, *The Coming of the Welfare State* (London, 1961), p.140.

Chapter 6: The Operation of the Poor Law in Belfast

1. John Boyle, *Leaders and Workers* (Dublin, 1961), p.59.
2. David Bleakley, *Saidie Patterson: Irish Peacemaker* (Belfast, 1980), p.4.
3. Brendan Walsh, *Religion and Demographic Behaviour in Ireland* (Dublin, 1968), p.7.
4. Interviews with Jack McNally, Tom Fitzpatrick and Cathal McCrystal, 1978.
5. *Ibid.*
6. *Ibid.*
7. *Ibid.*
8. St Vincent de Paul, Minute Books, 1920–40. Belfast and Dublin.
9. Board of Guardians Minutes, 10 November 1923.
10. Maurice Bruce, *The Coming of the Welfare State* (London, 1961), p.109.
11. House of Commons Debates (N.I.), II, col. 275, (29 March 1922).
12. *The Labour Opposition*, March 1925, (copies in Linen Hall Library, Belfast).
13. Board of Guardians Minutes, 19 January 1924.
14. *Ibid.,* 7 April 1924.

Chapter 7: The Guardians Kick Over the Traces

1. Board of Guardians Minutes, 14 January 1925.
2. *Ibid.*, 24 February 1925.
3. *Ibid.*, 31 March 1926.
4. *Ibid.*, 12 May 1926.
5. *House of Commons Debates* (N.I.), I, col. 1319 (17 May 1926).
6. Belfast newspapers, 14 June 1926.
7. Board of Guardians Minutes, 15 June 1926.
8. M. Bruce, *The Coming of the Welfare State* (London 1961), p.255.
9. Board of Guardians Minutes, 3 August 1927.
10. Bruce, *op. cit.*, p.277.
11. *House of Commons Debates* (N.I.), VIII, cols. 2244, 2247 (25 October 1927).
12. *Ibid.*, col. 4057 (8 December 1927).
13. *Ibid.*, col. 4071 (8 December 1927).
14. *Ibid.*, col. 4098 (8 December 1927).
15. Board of Guardians Minutes, 2 February 1928.
16. *Ibid.*, 4 June 1928.
17. *Ibid.*, 21 July 1928.
18. *Ibid.*, 31 July 1928.
19. *Ibid.*, 21 August 1928.
20. *Ibid.*, 30 October 1928.
21. *House of Commons Debates* (N.I.), IX, col. 4132 (6 December 1928).
22. Board of Guardians Minutes, 19 December 1928.
23. *Ibid.*, 8 January 1929.
24. *Ibid.*, 14 January 1929.
25. *Ibid.*, 15 January 1929.
26. *Ibid.*, 18 November 1929.
27. *House of Commons Debates* (N.I.), XI, col. 808 (25 June 1929).
28. *Ibid.*, X, col. 1670 (10 April 1929).
29. Board of Guardians Minutes, 14 January 1931.
30. *House of Commons Debates* (N.I.), X, col. 1670 (10 April 1929).
31. Board of Guardians Minutes, 5 May 1931.
32. *Ibid.*, 4 May 1931.
33. *Ibid.*, 19 May 1931.
34. *Ibid.*, 2 June 1931.

Chapter 8: Outdoor Relief riots 1932

1. Wal Harrington, *Unemployed Struggles 1919–1936* (London, 1936), p.233.
2. Board of Guardians Minutes, 8 February 1932.
3. Letter to Guardians, 13 April 1932.
4. Cabinet Minute 4/304/26 13 August 1932. Distress in N. Ireland.
5. Board of Guardians Minutes, 21 June 1932.
6. *House of Commons Debates* (N.I.), XIV, col. 180, (9 March 1932).
7. *Ibid.*, col. 109, (9 March 1932).
8. *Ibid.*, col. 553, (30 September 1932).
9. Board of Guardians Minutes, 20 August 1932.

Dispensaries	20 August 1932	Corresponding week 1931
1. Antrim	371 recipients	65 recipients
2. Antrim	474 recipients	83 recipients
3. Antrim	283 recipients	71 recipients
3a. Antrim	243 recipients	79 recipients
4. Antrim	353 recipients	104 recipients
5. Antrim	10 recipients	5 recipients
1. Down	429 recipients	90 recipients
2. Down	317 recipients	53 recipients
Total	2,480	550

10. *Ibid.*, 6 September 1932.
11. *Ibid.*, 30 August 1932.
12. Michael Farrell, *The Orange State*, (London, 1977), p.125.
13. Tom Bell, *The Struggle of the Unemployed in Belfast, Oct. 1932* (Cork, 1976).
14. Statement by David McLean, Socialist bookseller of Belfast in an interview in 1965.
15. Farrell, *op. cit.*, p.126.
16. Board of Guardians Minutes, 5 October 1932.
17. *Irish News*, 7 October 1932.
18. Board of Guardians Minutes, 8 October 1932.
19. *Ibid.*
20. *Ibid.*
21. Interview with Tom Fitzpatrick.
22. *Irish News*, 11 October 1932.
23. Cabinet Minutes 4/304/26 August 1932.
24. *Irish News*, 11 October 1932.
25. *Ibid.*, 12 October 1932.
26. James Kelly, *Capuchin Journal*, 1944.
27. *Irish News*, 14 October 1932.
28. Michael Farrell, *The Poor Law and the Workhouse in Belfast 1838–1948* (Belfast, 1978).
29. Board of Guardians Minuts, 13 October 1932.
30. Harrington, *op. cit.*
31. *Irish News*, 20 October 1932.
32. Board of Guardians Minutes, 19 October 1932.
33. *Ibid.*, 22 November 1932.
34. House of Commons Debates (N.I.), XV, col. 12 (22 November 1932).

Chapter 9: The Aftermath of the Riots

1. *Belfast News Letter*, 16 October 1932.
2. *Irish News*, 16 October 1932.
3. Michael Farrell, *The Orange State* (London, 1976), p.137.
4. Belinda Probert, *Beyond Orange and Green* (London, 1978), p.58.
5. Liam de Paor, *Divided Ulster* (London, 1970), p.105.
6. *Irish News*, 13 July 1933.
7. *Ibid.*
8. *Northern Whig*, 28 August 1933.
9. *Belfast News Letter* 25 March 1933.
10. George Gilmore, *Republican Congress* (Dublin, 1968), p.21.
11. Interviews with Jack Mairs and Dan McAllister, Belfast, June 1979. Dan McAllister took over William McMullen's position with the ITGWU in Belfast. Jack Mairs is a leading trade unionist in the Docks area.
12. *Belfast News Letter*, 23 July 1935.

Chapter 10: Old Wine, New Bottles

1. Board of Guardians Minutes, 17 February 1933.
2. *Ibid.*, 14 March 1933.
3. *Ibid.*, 16 March 1933.
4. *Ibid.*, 11 January 1934.
5. *Ibid.*, 9 April 1934.
6. *House of Commons Debates* (N.I.), XVI, col. 1904 (29 May 1934).
7. Board of Guardians Minutes, 3 January 1935.
8. *Ibid.*, 25 February 1935.
9. *House of Commons Debates* (N.I.), XVII, col. 831 (14 March 1935).
10. *Ibid.*, col. 849 (14 March 1935).
11. *Ibid.*, XVIII, col. 931, (1 April 1935).
12. *Ibid.*, col. 2342 (26 October 1936).
13. *Ibid.*, col. 648 (24 March 1936).
14. *Ibid.*, XIX, col. 595 (29 May 1936).
15. *Ibid.*, col. 1971 (14 October 1937).
16. *Ibid.*
17. *Ibid.*, col. 864 (20 April 1937).
18. Board of Guardians Minutes, 1 April 1938.
19. *Ibid.*, 24 May 1938.
20. *Ibid.*, 7 December 1938.
21. *Ibid.*, January to June 1939.

Chapter 11: The end of the Belfast Guardians

1. Buckland, *The Factory of Grievances* (Dublin, 1979), p.14.
2. Board of Guardians Minutes, 1 April 1938.
3. *Ibid.*, 19 July 1938.
4. *Ibid.*, 29 July 1938.
5. *Ibid.*, 7 September 1938.
6. *Ibid.*, 9 March 1939.

7. *House of Commons Debates* (N.I.), XXII, col. 800 (28 March 1939).
8. *Belfast Telegraph*, 20 March 1939.
9. *House of Commons Debates* (N.I.), XXII, col. 1104 (25 April 1939).
10. Buckland, *op. cit.*

Index

194